a passion for *tapas*

a passion for *tapas*

Love Food ® is an imprint of Parragon Books Ltd

Parragon
Queen Street House
4 Queen Street
Bath BA1 1HE, UK

Copyright © Parragon Books Ltd 2008

Love Food ® and the accompanying heart device is a trademark of Parragon Books Ltd

ISBN 978-1-4075-3139-7

Internal design by Jane Bozzard-Hill
Photography by Günter Beer and Laurie Evans
Home economy by Stevan Paul and Carol Tennant
Introduction by Beverly LeBlanc

Printed in Indonesia

Notes for the reader
This book uses imperial, metric, and US cup measurements. Follow the same units of
measurement throughout; do not mix imperial and metric. All spoon measurements are
level, unless otherwise stated: teaspoons are assumed to be 5 ml, and tablespoons are
assumed to be 15 ml. Unless otherwise stated, milk is assumed to be whole, eggs and
individual fruits such as bananas are medium, and pepper is freshly ground black pepper.

Recipes using raw or very lightly cooked eggs should be avoided by infants, the elderly,
pregnant women, convalescents, and anyone with a chronic condition. Pregnant and
breast-feeding women are advised to avoid eating peanuts and peanut products.

contents

Introduction   6

Vegetables, Nuts & Olives   12

Meat & Poultry   62

Fish & Seafood   110

Eggs & Cheese   158

Bread   206

Index   254

Introduction

Welcome to the world of Spanish tapas culture. Tapas are small, bite-size

morsels of tasty food, which are uniquely Spanish. Tapas are served in Spanish bars

and cafés throughout the day, and the preparation, eating, and enjoyment of tapas

are essential parts of everyday Spanish life. It can be tempting to describe tapas

as the Spanish version of French hors d'oeuvres or Mediterranean meze, but they

are very different. Unlike meze, for example, tapas are never intended to replace a

proper meal, nor do they form the first course of a meal, as do hors d'oeuvres.

"Tapas are a national obsession of endless variety"

The Spanish rarely drink alcohol without eating, so wherever you travel in this vast country you will find people standing at bars nibbling bite-size meat-, poultry-, vegetable-, and seafood-based tapas with their drinks, be it late morning, lunchtime, mid-afternoon, or in the evening before going home for a late supper. Older Spaniards fondly remember when simple tapas—a bowl of almonds or olives, slices of bread drizzled with olive oil, or chunks of chorizo—were always served free with any drink. That tradition, unfortunately, hasn't stood the test of time, but there hasn't been any decline in the popularity of tapas themselves.

The Spanish word *tapa* means "lid," and the nation's obsession with these flavorsome tidbits began hundreds of years ago when Andalusian innkeepers used slices of bread to keep dust and bugs out of the glasses of wine and sherry provided for passing horsemen. Eventually slices of ham and cheese were added to the bread, and tapas as we know them today were born, evolving from the arid landscape of southern Spain into a national obsession of endless variety. In fact, sampling a selection of tapas is a good overall introduction to the exciting flavors of Spanish cuisine.

Tapas bars are called tascas, and they are very egalitarian establishments, where wine barons, bankers, and industrialists rub shoulders with farm workers, students, parents with children, and even tourists. Unlike American bars or English pubs, however, the raison d'être of tapas bars puts conversations and rendez-vous ahead of simply drinking. Tapas bars always have a convivial atmosphere with a background buzz of friends and neighbors meeting, greeting, and chatting.

If the bar is in a tourist area you might be given a menu, often with photographs to overcome language problems, but otherwise don't expect one. Some tapas bars list the daily offerings on a chalkboard, or you make your selection from the prepared tapas displayed in glass cabinets on the bar. In most of Spain the bartender or a waiter or waitress will serve you, but in the Basque Country it is traditional for customers to help themselves.

As universal as the word *tapas* is, not all tapas are the same, as there are several categories. *Cosas de picar*, which literally means "little things to nibble" are the simplest, such as a bowl of salted almonds, olives, or cubes of cheese. These are, of course, the easiest tapas for you to serve with drinks before dinner. *Pinchos*, however, can be a bit more substantial and are easily recognized because they are speared with flat wooden toothpicks called *banderillas*, which resemble the darts used in bullfighting. *Cazuelas*, a type of tapas with a sauce and often hot, are so called because they are usually served in the small, brown glazed earthenware dishes also called *cazuelas*. Sizzling Chile Shrimp (see page 138), Chicken Livers in Sherry Sauce (see page 104), and Fava Beans with Ham (see page 42) are examples of popular *cazuelas*. These are ideal to serve to guests with drinks before dinner when you don't want to serve a first course at the table. *Montaditos* is the word to describe slices of French bread generously topped with mayonnaise-based salads, such as potato salad, tuna salad (see page 230), or salt cod (see page 216), which are served throughout the country. Part of the popularity of this type of tapas has to be that they are inexpensive and easy to prepare. *Bocadillos*, on the other hand, are small, more conventional sandwiches with a simple filling between two slices of bread. Roast loin of pork, cured ham, spicy sausage, cheese, and thin omelets are typical fillings. *Rebozadas* are the fried fritters Spaniards are so fond of—try Zucchini Fritters with a Dipping Sauce (see page 26).

"Tapas culture is most obvious in larger cities"

By convention tapas aren't intended to be a meal, but when you see a tapas described as a *racione*, it will be more filling than most and could be just what you are looking for at lunchtime to accompany a glass of chilled *vino blanco*.

As you look through the recipes in this book, you'll see that preparing tapas offers plenty of scope for experimentation and that they can be assembled from the simplest pantry ingredients (see page 11). Tapas are particularly suited to entertaining, because they can be made well in advance, so you can enjoy the gathering as much as your guests.

Tapas Culture

You'll find tapas in every small village or town, but the height of tapas culture is most obvious in larger cities, where the nightly pilgrimage from tapas bar to tapas bar is called *tapeo*. It's a slow, relaxed procession as friends congregate at one bar to catch up on the day's news over a small glass of *fino* sherry, wine, or a chilled draft beer with, perhaps, a crisp, deep-fried salt-cod fritter or a slice of tortilla, before casually meandering on to the next bar for more conversation, another drink, and perhaps a few cubes of sizzling chorizo or fried, batter-coated squid rings. It's all part of the ebb and flow of the evening that a bar can be packed like a sardine can and then be virtually empty 30 minutes later, before filling up again.

Of course, regional specialties change as you travel across the country, but some tapas you will find everywhere include Spanish Tortilla, a thick egg and potato omelet; crisp, deep-fried zucchini; wafer-thin slices of Serrano ham; finely diced potato salad to spread on slices of bread; and bowls of salted, toasted almonds.

Seville and the other Andalucian cities of Granada, Cadiz, and Cordoba have a lively tapas tradition, but the *tapeo* is also part of living and working in Madrid and San Sebastian. The small, winding streets behind Madrid's Plaza Mayor are where the locals gather for their nightly tapas.

In the northern Basque Country all food, be it simple marinated anchovy fillets on bread or a three-course meal in a Michelin-starred restaurant, is taken seriously, very seriously indeed. Not surprisingly, tapas in the stylish city of San Sebastian are unlike anywhere else. For a start, the nightly bar crawl is *txikiteo* and tapas are called *pintxos*, the Basque word for *pinchos*, because they are almost always speared with a toothpick. Even a slice of tortilla is served on bread with a toothpick securing the two ingredients together.

Bars in the oldest part of San Sebastian compete to see which can offer the most tempting selection. It's not unusual to see thirty or more platters of tapas arranged on the bar with small wooden stands, like cake stands, used to create extra space for a second layer of platters.

When you order your drink at the bar, just ask for a plate and make your selection from all the appetizing-looking morsels. For a taste of Basque cuisine, try Anchovy Rolls (see page 228), Salt Cod on Garlic Toasts (see page 216), Basque Scrambled Eggs (see page 180), and Deep-Fried Green Chiles (see page 20). When you are ready to move on to the next bar, the barman will simply count the number of toothpicks on your plate to calculate your bill. If you want to look like a local, throw your paper napkins onto the floor.

Interestingly, Barcelona, Spain's second largest city and capital of Catalunya, doesn't have a long history of tapas culture. It is only in recent years, as improved transportation and communications have blurred regional distinctions throughout the country, not just in Catalunya, that large tapas bars have appeared. Look for the bars called *xampanyerias*. Once unique to Barcelona, these bars specialize in tapas and cava, the Spanish sparkling wine.

"Recreate the flavors of Spain's tapas bars at home"

One of the great joys of tapas is that they are easy to prepare and can be made using ingredients that are widely available—in fact, it is likely that you will have many of them in your pantry already. However, it is worth hunting out some of the more unusual items— these can be purchased from large supermarkets or gourmet food stores. The following ingredients will help you to recreate the flavors of Spain's tapas bars at home.

Almonds *(almendras)* A bowl of blanched almonds is one of the easiest tapas you can serve, but if you want to be more ambitious, try Salted Almonds (see page 14) or Tiny Meatballs in Almond Sauce (see page 72). For freshness, buy unblanched and blanch just before using—just drop the nuts in boiling water for a few minutes, then drain and refresh under cold water. Use your fingers to squeeze the nuts so they pop out of the skins.

Cheese *(queso)* Many of Spain's numerous cheeses feature in tapas selections. For a simple tapas, serve slices of Manchego, a sheep's milk cheese from La Mancha, or cubes of Cabrales, a rich blue cheese, with drinks. Croquettes are a thrifty way to make use of the small pieces of leftover cheese.

Cured meats *(charcutería)* Spanish tapas cooks make great use of cured pork, lamb, and beef, and anyone visiting Spain for the first time will be dazzled by the quantity of packets in supermarkets, sliced and ready for putting on plates for serving. Serrano or mountain ham *(jamón serrano)*, perhaps the best known, features at many tapas bars—it can be served in thin slices, as a sandwich filling, or on bread topped with vegetables. Prosciutto makes a good substitute. Plain cooked ham is *jamón cocida*, also used in tapas. The most highly regarded will be labeled as Iberico, and you'll recognize it by the hefty price. Other less well known, but equally popular, charcuterie include boneless pork loin *(lomo)* and Spain's ubiquitous pork sausage, the spicy chorizo, colored with paprika.

Garlic *(ajo)* An essential Spanish flavoring. Buy fresh and use within a month once the head has been broken into.

Legumes *(legumbres secas)* Spanish kitchen cupboards contain many jars and tins of legumes, including lima beans *(alubia de Perú)*, chickpeas *(garbanzos)*, and lentils *(lentejas)*, ready to use without having to go to the trouble of overnight soaking and boiling first. Chickpeas & Chorizo (see page 90) is a typical tapas, bursting with flavor and easy to prepare.

Olive oil *(aceite de oliva)* Spain is the world's largest olive oil producer, so it is a regular feature of Spanish cooking; butter is rarely used. Heat destroys the flavor of oil so save your best, and most expensive, extra virgin oil for uncooked dishes and cook with plain olive oil.

Paprika *(pimentón)* Made from ground, dried red peppers, paprika adds a mild or strong smoky flavor and vibrant red color to dishes. It's one of the essential flavors of chorizo and many Spanish dishes.

Pimientos del piquillo Take a tip from Spanish cooks and always keep a jar of these grilled and skinned bell peppers in your pantry. They come bottled in olive oil or brine, either whole or sliced, and take the work out of serving roasted bell peppers.

Saffron *(azafrán)* Good-quality Spanish saffron comes from La Mancha and is expensive. Saffron Shrimp with Lemon Mayonnaise (see page 140) is a good recipe to showcase the spice's unrivaled golden color and distinctive flavor. Enhance the flavor by lightly toasting before using. Store in a sealed container.

Canned fish There is a wide range of preserved fish available, including anchovies *(boquerones)*, sardines *(sardines)*, and tuna *(atún)*. Buy fish preserved in olive oil for the best flavor.

vegetables, nuts & olives

Tapas bars can be a culinary heaven for vegetable lovers in Spain, a land of serious meat eaters. This chapter contains a wealth of vegetable recipes, celebrating Spain's position as gardener to Europe. Chargrilled bell peppers and zucchini always add color and flavor to tapas menus.

Spanish cooks never run out of ideas for preparing potatoes, but Patatas Bravas, so called because of the hot chili sauce, is one of the country's favorite tapas. Try it and you'll understand why.

Finally, what could be more quintessentially Spanish than nibbling a bowl of Olives with Orange & Lemon while sipping a cold drink?

salted almonds

SERVES 6–8
as part of a tapas meal

8 oz/225 g whole almonds,
   in their skins or blanched
4 tbsp Spanish olive oil
1 tsp paprika or ground cumin
   (optional)
coarse sea salt

Preheat the oven to 350°F/180°C. Fresh almonds in their skins are superior in taste, but blanched almonds are much more convenient. If the almonds are not blanched, place them in a large bowl, cover with boiling water for 3–4 minutes, then drain and plunge them into cold water for 1 minute. Drain them well in a strainer, then slide off the skins between your fingers. Dry the almonds well on paper towels.

Put the oil in a roasting pan and swirl it around so that it covers the base. Add the almonds and toss them in the pan so that they are evenly coated in the oil, then spread them out in a single layer.

Roast the almonds in the preheated oven for 20 minutes, or until they are light golden brown, tossing several times during the cooking. Drain the almonds on paper towels, then transfer them to a bowl.

While the almonds are still warm, sprinkle with plenty of sea salt and paprika, if using, and toss together to coat. Serve the almonds warm or cold. The almonds are at their best when served freshly cooked so, if possible, cook them on the day that you plan to eat them. However, they can be stored in an airtight container for up to 3 days.

spicy cracked marinated olives

SERVES 8
as part of a tapas meal

2¹/₂ cups canned or jarred large
   green Spanish olives, drained
4 garlic cloves, peeled
2 tsp coriander seeds
1 small lemon
4 fresh thyme sprigs
4 feathery stalks of fennel
2 small fresh red chiles
   (optional)
Spanish extra virgin olive oil
pepper

If using unpitted olives, place them on a cutting board and, using a rolling pin, bash them lightly so that they crack slightly. Alternatively, use a sharp knife to cut a lengthwise slit in each olive as far as the pit. Using the flat side of a broad knife, lightly crush each garlic clove. Using a mortar and pestle, crack the coriander seeds. Cut the lemon, with its rind, into small chunks.

Place the olives, garlic, coriander seeds, lemon chunks, thyme sprigs, fennel, and chiles, if using, in a large bowl and toss together. Season with pepper to taste, but you should not need to add salt as canned or jarred olives are usually salty enough. Pack the ingredients tightly into a glass jar with a lid. Pour in enough olive oil to cover the olives, then seal the jar tightly.

Let the olives stand at room temperature for 24 hours, then marinate in the refrigerator for at least 1 week but preferably 2 weeks before serving. Give the jar a gentle shake occasionally to re-mix the ingredients. Return the olives to room temperature and remove from the oil to serve. Provide wooden toothpicks for spearing the olives.

olives with orange & lemon

Dry-roast the fennel seeds and cumin seeds in a small, heavy-bottom skillet, shaking the skillet frequently, until they begin to pop and give off their aroma. Remove the skillet from the heat and let cool.

Place the olives, orange and lemon rind, shallots, cinnamon, and roasted seeds in a bowl.

Whisk the vinegar, oil, orange juice, mint, and parsley together in a bowl and pour over the olives. Toss well, then cover and let chill for 1–2 days before serving.

SERVES 4–6
as part of a tapas meal

2 tsp fennel seeds
2 tsp cumin seeds
1$\frac{1}{4}$ cups green Spanish olives
1$\frac{1}{4}$ cups black Spanish olives
2 tsp grated orange rind
2 tsp grated lemon rind
3 shallots, finely chopped
pinch of ground cinnamon
4 tbsp white wine vinegar
5 tbsp Spanish extra virgin
   olive oil
2 tbsp orange juice
1 tbsp chopped fresh mint
1 tbsp chopped fresh parsley

deep-fried green chiles

SERVES 4–6
as part of a tapas meal

Spanish olive oil, for frying
9 oz/250 g sweet or hot fresh
   chiles
sea salt

Heat 3 inches/7.5 cm of oil in a large, heavy-bottom saucepan until it reaches 350–375°F/180–190°C, or until a cube of bread turns brown in 30 seconds.

Rinse the chiles and pat them very dry with paper towels. Drop them in the hot oil for no longer than 20 seconds, or until they turn bright green and the skins blister.

Remove with a slotted spoon and drain well on crumpled paper towels. Sprinkle with sea salt and serve immediately.

sautéed garlic mushrooms

SERVES 6
as part of a tapas meal

1 lb/450 g button mushrooms
5 tbsp Spanish olive oil
2 garlic cloves, finely chopped
lemon juice
4 tbsp chopped fresh parsley
salt and pepper
lemon wedges, to garnish
crusty bread, to serve

Wipe or brush clean the mushrooms, then trim the stems. Cut any large mushrooms in half or into quarters. Heat the oil in a large, heavy-bottom skillet. Add the garlic and cook for 30–60 seconds, or until lightly browned. Add the mushrooms and sauté over high heat, stirring frequently, until the mushrooms have absorbed all the oil in the skillet.

Reduce the heat to low. When the juices have come out of the mushrooms, increase the heat again and sauté for 4–5 minutes, stirring frequently, until the juices have almost evaporated. Add a squeeze of lemon juice and season with salt and pepper to taste. Stir in the parsley and cook for an additional minute.

Transfer the sautéed mushrooms to a warmed serving dish, then garnish with lemon wedges and serve piping hot or warm. Accompany with crusty bread for mopping up the juices.

chile mushrooms

Heat the butter with the olive oil in a large, heavy-bottom skillet. When the butter has melted, add the mushrooms, garlic, and chile and cook over medium–low heat, stirring frequently, for 5 minutes.

Stir in the lemon juice and season with salt and pepper to taste.

Transfer to warmed serving dishes and serve immediately, garnished with parsley sprigs.

SERVES 6–8
as part of a tapas meal

1/2 stick butter
5 tbsp olive oil
2 lb 4 oz/1 kg white mushrooms
4 fat garlic cloves, finely chopped
1 fresh red chile, seeded and finely chopped
1 tbsp lemon juice
salt and pepper
fresh parsley sprigs, to garnish

zucchini fritters
with a dipping sauce

SERVES 6–8
as part of a tapas meal

1 lb/450 g baby zucchini
3 tbsp all-purpose flour
1 tsp paprika
1 large egg
2 tbsp milk
corn oil, for frying
coarse sea salt

pine nut sauce
$2/3$ cup pine nuts
1 garlic clove, peeled
3 tbsp Spanish extra virgin
    olive oil
1 tbsp lemon juice
3 tbsp water
1 tbsp chopped fresh flat-leaf
    parsley
salt and pepper

To make the pine nut sauce, place the pine nuts and garlic in a food processor and process to form a puree. With the motor still running, gradually add the olive oil, lemon juice, and water to form a smooth sauce. Stir in the parsley and season with salt and pepper to taste. Transfer to a serving bowl and reserve until needed.

To prepare the zucchini, cut them on the diagonal into thin slices about $1/4$ inch/5 mm thick. Place the flour and paprika in a plastic bag and mix together. Beat the egg and milk together in a large bowl.

Add the zucchini slices to the flour mixture and toss well together until coated. Shake off the excess flour. Heat the corn oil in a large, heavy-bottom skillet to a depth of about $1/2$ inch/1 cm. Dip the zucchini slices, one at a time, into the egg mixture, then slip them into the hot oil. Cook the zucchini slices in batches in a single layer so that they do not overcrowd the skillet, for 2 minutes, or until they are crisp and golden brown.

Using a slotted spoon, remove the zucchini fritters from the skillet and drain on paper towels. Continue until all the zucchini slices have been fried.

Serve the zucchini fritters piping hot, lightly sprinkled with sea salt, and accompanied by the pine nut sauce for dipping.

deep-fried artichoke hearts

SERVES 4–6
as part of a tapas meal

1/2 cup self-rising flour
1/4 tsp salt
1/4 tsp hot or sweet smoked
   Spanish paprika
1 garlic clove, crushed
5 tbsp water
1 tbsp olive oil
juice of 1/2 lemon
12 small globe artichokes
sunflower or Spanish olive oil,
   for deep-frying
Aïoli (see page 58), to serve

To make the batter, put the flour, salt, paprika, and garlic in a large bowl and make a well in the center. Gradually pour the water and oil into the well and mix in the flour mixture from the side, beating continuously, until all the flour is incorporated and a smooth batter forms. Let rest while preparing the artichokes.

Fill a bowl with cold water and add the lemon juice. Cut off the stalks of the artichokes. With your hands, break off all the leaves and carefully remove the choke (the mass of silky hairs) by pulling it out with your fingers or scooping it out with a spoon. Immediately put the artichoke hearts in the acidulated water to prevent discoloration.

Bring a saucepan of lightly salted water to a boil, add the artichoke hearts, and cook for 15 minutes, or until tender but still firm, then drain well and pat dry with paper towels.

Heat enough oil in a deep-fat fryer to 350–375°F/180–190°C, or until a cube of bread browns in 30 seconds. Spear an artichoke heart on a toothpick and dip into the batter, then drop the artichoke heart and toothpick into the hot oil. Cook the artichoke hearts, in batches to avoid overcrowding, for 1–2 minutes, or until golden brown and crisp. Remove with a slotted spoon or draining basket and drain on paper towels.

Serve hot, accompanied by a bowl of aïoli for dipping.

artichoke hearts
& asparagus

Trim and discard the coarse, woody ends of the asparagus spears. Make sure all the stems are about the same length, then tie them together loosely with clean kitchen string. If you have an asparagus steamer, you don't need to tie the stems together—just place them in the basket.

Bring a tall saucepan of lightly salted water to a boil. Add the asparagus, making sure that the tips are protruding above the water, then reduce the heat and let simmer for 10–15 minutes, or until tender. Test by piercing a stem just above the water level with the point of a sharp knife. Drain, then refresh under cold running water and drain again.

Cut the asparagus spears into 1-inch/2.5-cm pieces, keeping the tips intact. Cut the artichoke hearts into small wedges and combine with the asparagus in a bowl.

Whisk the orange juice, orange rind, oil, and mustard together in a bowl and season with salt and pepper to taste. If serving immediately, pour the dressing over the artichoke hearts and asparagus and toss lightly.

Arrange the salad greens in individual serving dishes and top with the artichoke and asparagus mixture. Serve immediately. Alternatively, store the salad, covered, in the refrigerator and add the dressing just before serving.

SERVES 4–6
as part of a tapas meal

1 lb/450 g asparagus spears
14 oz/400 g canned artichoke hearts, drained and rinsed
2 tbsp freshly squeezed orange juice
1/2 tsp finely grated orange rind
2 tbsp walnut oil
1 tsp Dijon mustard
salt and pepper
salad greens, to serve

marinated eggplants

SERVES 4
as part of a tapas meal

2 eggplants, halved lengthwise
4 tbsp Spanish olive oil
2 garlic cloves, finely chopped
2 tbsp chopped fresh parsley
1 tbsp chopped fresh thyme
2 tbsp lemon juice
salt and pepper

Make 3–4 slashes in the flesh of the eggplant halves and place, cut-side down, in an ovenproof dish. Season with salt and pepper to taste, then pour over the oil and sprinkle with the garlic, parsley, and thyme. Cover and let marinate at room temperature for 2–3 hours.

Preheat the oven to 350°F/180°C. Uncover the dish and roast the eggplants in the preheated oven for 45 minutes. Remove the dish from the oven and turn over the eggplants. Baste with the cooking juices and sprinkle with the lemon juice. Return to the oven and cook for an additional 15 minutes.

Transfer the eggplants to serving plates. Spoon over the cooking juices and serve hot or warm.

pickled stuffed sweet peppers

SERVES 6
as part of a tapas meal

7 oz/200 g Cuajada cheese,
  Queso del Tietar or other
  fresh goat cheese
14 oz/400 g pickled sweet
  peppers or pimientos del
  piquillo, drained
1 tbsp finely chopped fresh dill
salt and pepper

Cut the cheese into pieces about $1/2$ inch/1 cm long. Slit the sides of the sweet peppers and seed, if you like. Stuff the peppers with the cheese.

Arrange the stuffed peppers on serving plates. Sprinkle with the dill and season with salt and pepper to taste. Cover and chill until ready to serve.

stuffed cherry tomatoes

If necessary, cut and discard a very thin slice from the stem end of each tomato to make the bases flat and stable. Cut a thin slice from the smooth end of each cherry tomato and discard. Using a serrated knife or teaspoon, loosen the pulp and seeds of each and scoop out, discarding the flesh. Turn the scooped-out tomatoes upside down on paper towels and let drain for 5 minutes.

To make the anchovy and olive filling, drain the anchovies, reserving the oil for later, then chop finely and place in a bowl. Add the olives and hard-cooked eggs. Pour in a trickle of the reserved olive oil to moisten the mixture, then season with pepper. (Don't add salt to season, as the anchovies are salty.) Mix well together.

To make the crab mayonnaise filling, place the crabmeat, mayonnaise, and parsley in a bowl and mix well together. Season the filling with salt and pepper to taste. Sprinkle with paprika before serving.

To make the black olive and caper filling, place the olives and capers on paper towels to drain them well, then chop finely and place in a bowl. Add the aïoli and mix well together. Season the filling with salt and pepper to taste.

Fill a pastry bag fitted with a 3/4-inch/2-cm plain tip with the filling of your choice and use to fill the hollow tomato shells. Store the cherry tomatoes in the refrigerator until ready to serve.

SERVES 8
as part of a tapas meal

24 cherry tomatoes

anchovy & olive filling
1 3/4 oz/50 g canned anchovy
   fillets in olive oil
8 pimiento-stuffed green
   Spanish olives, finely chopped
2 large hard-cooked eggs,
   finely chopped
pepper

crab mayonnaise filling
6 oz/175 g canned crabmeat,
   drained
4 tbsp mayonnaise
1 tbsp chopped fresh flat-leaf
   parsley
salt and pepper
paprika, to garnish

black olive & caper filling
12 pitted black Spanish olives
3 tbsp capers
6 tbsp Aïoli (see page 58)
salt and pepper

simmered summer vegetables

SERVES 6–8
as part of a tapas meal

1 large eggplant
4 tbsp Spanish olive oil
1 onion, thinly sliced
2 garlic cloves, finely chopped
2 zucchini, thinly sliced
1 red bell pepper, cored,
    seeded, and thinly sliced
1 green bell pepper, cored,
    seeded, and thinly sliced
8 tomatoes, peeled, seeded,
    and chopped
salt and pepper
chopped fresh flat-leaf parsley,
    to garnish
slices thick country bread,
    to serve (optional)

Cut the eggplant into 1-inch/2.5-cm cubes. Heat the oil in a large ovenproof casserole, then add the onion and cook over medium heat, stirring occasionally, for 5 minutes, or until softened but not browned. Add the garlic and cook, stirring, for 30 seconds, or until softened.

Increase the heat to medium–high, then add the eggplant cubes and cook, stirring occasionally, for 10 minutes, or until softened and beginning to brown. Add the zucchini and bell peppers and cook, stirring occasionally, for 10 minutes, or until softened. Add the tomatoes and season with salt and pepper to taste.

Bring the mixture to a boil, then reduce the heat, cover, and simmer, stirring occasionally so that the vegetables do not stick to the bottom of the casserole, for 15–20 minutes, or until tender. If necessary, uncover, then increase the heat and cook to evaporate any excess liquid, as the mixture should be thick.

Serve hot or cold, garnished with chopped parsley and accompanied by bread slices, if using, for scooping up the vegetables.

green beans with pine nuts

SERVES 8
as part of a tapas meal

2 tbsp Spanish olive oil
scant $1/3$ cup pine nuts
$1/2$–1 tsp paprika
1 lb/450 g green beans
1 small onion, finely chopped
1 garlic clove, finely chopped
juice of $1/2$ lemon
salt and pepper

Heat the oil in a large, heavy-bottom skillet, add the pine nuts and cook for about 1 minute, stirring all the time and shaking the skillet, until light golden brown. Using a slotted spoon, remove the pine nuts from the skillet, drain well on paper towels, then transfer to a bowl. Set aside the oil in the skillet for later. Add the paprika, according to taste, to the pine nuts, stir together until coated, and then set aside.

Trim the green beans and remove any strings if necessary. Put the beans in a saucepan, pour over boiling water, return to a boil, and cook for 5 minutes, or until tender but still firm. Drain well in a strainer.

Reheat the oil in the skillet, add the onion and cook for 5–10 minutes, or until softened and starting to brown. Add the garlic and cook for an additional 30 seconds.

Add the beans to the skillet and cook for 2–3 minutes, tossing together with the onion until heated through. Season the beans with salt and pepper to taste.

Turn the contents of the skillet into a warmed serving dish, sprinkle over the lemon juice, and toss together. Sprinkle over the golden pine nuts and serve hot.

fava beans with ham

Bring a large saucepan of lightly salted water to a boil. Add the beans and continue to boil for 5–10 minutes until just tender. Drain and put in a bowl of cold water to stop additional cooking. Unless the beans are young and tiny, peel off the outer skins.

Meanwhile, heat 1 tablespoon of the oil in a skillet over medium–high heat. Add the onion and cook for about 5 minutes until softened, but not browned. Add the beans.

Stir in the ham and parsley and check the seasoning; the meat is salty, so don't add salt until after tasting. Transfer to a serving bowl and drizzle with the remaining oil. Serve at room temperature with slices of French bread.

**SERVES 4–6
as part of a tapas meal**

1/2 cup fresh or frozen shelled
   fava beans
2 tbsp Spanish olive oil
1 Spanish red onion, very finely
   chopped
1 slice medium-thick serrano
   ham or prosciutto, chopped
finely chopped fresh parsley,
   to taste
salt and pepper
French bread, to serve

baby leek & asparagus salad

SERVES 6
as part of a tapas meal

3 eggs
1 lb/450 g baby leeks, trimmed
8 oz/225 g fresh young
    asparagus spears, trimmed
2/3 cup mayonnaise
2 tbsp sherry vinegar
1 garlic clove, crushed
salt and pepper
2 tbsp capers, to garnish

Put the eggs in a saucepan, then cover with cold water and slowly bring to a boil. Reduce the heat and simmer gently for 10 minutes. Immediately drain the eggs and rinse under cold running water to cool. Gently tap the eggs to crack the shells and let stand until cold.

Meanwhile, slice the leeks and asparagus into about 3 1/2-inch/9-cm lengths. Put both vegetables in a saucepan of boiling water, then return to a boil and boil for 12 minutes, or until just tender. Drain and rinse under cold running water, then drain well.

Put the mayonnaise in a large bowl. Add the vinegar and garlic, then mix together until smooth. Season with salt and pepper to taste. Add the leeks and asparagus to the dressing and toss together until well coated. Transfer the vegetables to a serving dish, then cover and chill in the refrigerator for at least 1 hour.

Just before serving, crack the shells of the eggs all over and remove them. Slice the eggs into quarters and add to the salad. Sprinkle over the capers and serve.

zucchini salad
with cilantro dressing

SERVES 6
as part of a tapas meal

1 lb 2 oz/500 g small zucchini
1 tsp salt
1 tbsp Spanish olive oil
1 garlic clove, crushed
1/3 cup pine nuts

cilantro dressing
2 garlic cloves, chopped
1 tsp ground cumin
1/2 cup chopped fresh cilantro
    leaves
2 tbsp chopped fresh flat-leaf
    parsley
5 tbsp Spanish extra virgin
    olive oil
2 tbsp white wine vinegar
salt and pepper

Thinly slice the zucchini lengthwise. Layer the slices in a colander, sprinkling over a little salt, and set over a large plate. Let drain for about 1 hour.

Meanwhile, make the dressing. Put the garlic, cumin, and herbs in a food processor and pulse until well mixed.

With the motor running, add 1 tablespoon of the extra virgin olive oil, drop by drop. Using a spatula, scrape down the side of the bowl. With the motor running again, very slowly add the remaining oil in a thin, steady stream until it has all been incorporated and the dressing has thickened slightly. Add the vinegar to the dressing and process for 1 minute, or until blended. Season with salt and pepper to taste.

When the zucchini have drained, quickly rinse the slices under cold running water, then dry well with paper towels or a clean dish towel. Put in a large bowl and add the olive oil and garlic, then toss together lightly.

Heat a ridged grill pan. Add the zucchini slices, in batches in a single layer, and cook, turning once, for 5 minutes, or until tender. Transfer to a large serving bowl. Set aside and let cool slightly.

Sprinkle the pine nuts over the zucchini. If the dressing has separated, whisk it together, then drizzle some over the zucchini. Serve the zucchini accompanied by the remaining dressing in a small serving bowl.

summer salad in a tomato dressing

Put the eggs (if using) in a saucepan, then cover with cold water and slowly bring to a boil. Reduce the heat and simmer gently for 10 minutes. Immediately drain the eggs and rinse under cold running water to cool. Gently tap the eggs to crack the shells and let stand until cold.

Meanwhile, cut the beans into 1-inch/2.5-cm lengths. Bring a saucepan of lightly salted water to a boil, add the beans, and cook for 2 minutes, then drain well. Rinse under cold running water and let stand until cold.

To make the dressing, coarsely grate the tomatoes into a food processor, discarding the skins left in your hands. Add the garlic, oil, vinegar, paprika, and sugar and process until smooth. Season with salt to taste.

Put the cooled beans in a large serving bowl. Add the tomatoes and bell peppers and toss the vegetables together. Drizzle the dressing over the vegetables.

Sprinkle the gherkins, olives, and capers into the salad. Just before serving, crack the shells of the eggs all over and remove them. Slice the eggs into quarters and add to the salad.

SERVES 8
as part of a tapas meal

4 eggs (optional)
3 1/2 oz/100 g fine green beans
1 lb 2 oz/500 g cherry or baby
 plum tomatoes
1 green bell pepper, cored,
 seeded, and diced
1 yellow bell pepper, cored,
 seeded, and diced
4 small gherkins, sliced
heaping 1/4 cup pitted black
 Spanish olives, halved
1 tsp capers

tomato dressing
6 firm tomatoes
1 garlic clove, chopped
6 tbsp Spanish extra virgin
 olive oil
3 tbsp sherry vinegar
1/2 tsp hot or sweet smoked
 Spanish paprika
pinch of sugar
salt

roasted bell pepper salad

SERVES 8
as part of a tapas meal

3 red bell peppers
3 yellow bell peppers
5 tbsp Spanish extra virgin
    olive oil
2 tbsp dry sherry vinegar or
    lemon juice
2 garlic cloves, crushed
pinch of sugar
1 tbsp capers
8 small black Spanish olives
2 tbsp chopped fresh marjoram,
    plus extra sprigs to garnish
salt and pepper

Preheat the broiler. Place all the bell peppers on a wire rack or broiler pan and cook under a hot broiler for 10 minutes, turning them frequently, until their skins have blackened and blistered.

Remove the roasted bell peppers from the heat, then place them in a bowl and immediately cover tightly with a clean, damp dish towel. Alternatively, place the bell peppers in a plastic bag. You will find that the steam helps to soften the skins and makes it easier to remove them. Let the bell peppers stand for about 15 minutes, or until they are cool enough to handle.

Holding 1 bell pepper at a time over a clean bowl, use a sharp knife to make a small hole in the base and gently squeeze out the juices and reserve them. Still holding the bell pepper over the bowl, carefully peel off the skin with your fingers or a knife and discard it. Cut the bell peppers in half and remove the stem, core, and seeds, then cut each bell pepper into neat thin strips. Arrange the bell pepper strips attractively on a serving dish.

Add the olive oil, sherry vinegar, garlic, sugar, and salt and pepper to taste to the reserved pepper juices. Whisk together until combined, then drizzle the dressing over the salad.

Sprinkle the capers, olives, and chopped marjoram over the salad, then garnish with marjoram sprigs and serve at room temperature.

orange & fennel salad

SERVES 4
as part of a tapas meal

4 large, juicy oranges
1 large fennel bulb, very thinly
  sliced
1 mild white onion, finely sliced
2 tbsp Spanish extra virgin
  olive oil
12 plump black Spanish olives,
  pitted and thinly sliced
1 fresh red chile, seeded and
  very thinly sliced (optional)
finely chopped fresh parsley
French bread, to serve

Finely grate the rind from the oranges into a bowl and reserve. Using a small, serrated knife, remove all the white pith from the oranges, working over a bowl to catch the juices. Cut the oranges horizontally into thin slices.

Toss the orange slices with the fennel and onion slices. Whisk the olive oil into the reserved orange juice, then spoon over the oranges. Sprinkle the olive slices over the top, add the chile, if using, then sprinkle with the orange rind and parsley. Serve with slices of French bread.

a salad of melon, chorizo
& artichokes

To prepare the artichokes, cut off the stalks. With your hands, break off the toughest outer leaves at the base until the tender inside leaves are visible. Using a pair of scissors, cut the spiky tips off the leaves. Using a sharp knife, pare the dark green skin from the base and down the stem. As you prepare them, brush the cut surfaces of the artichokes with lemon juice to prevent discoloration. Carefully remove the choke (the mass of silky hairs) by pulling it out with your fingers or by scooping it out with a spoon. It is very important to remove all the choke as the little barbs, if eaten, can irritate the throat. However, if you are using very young artichokes, you do not need to worry about removing the choke and you can include the stalk too, well scraped, as it will be quite tender. Cut the artichokes into quarters and brush them again with lemon juice.

Heat the olive oil in a large, heavy-bottom skillet, then add the prepared artichokes and cook, stirring frequently, for 5 minutes, or until the artichoke leaves are golden brown. Remove from the skillet, transfer to a large serving bowl, and let cool.

To prepare the melon, cut in half and scoop out the seeds with a spoon. Cut the flesh into bite-size cubes. Add to the cooled artichokes. Cut the chorizo into bite-size chunks and add to the melon and artichokes.

To make the dressing, put all the ingredients in a small bowl and whisk together. Just before serving, pour the dressing over the prepared salad ingredients and toss together. Serve the salad garnished with tarragon or parsley sprigs.

SERVES 8
as part of a tapas meal

12 small globe artichokes
juice of 1/2 lemon
2 tbsp Spanish olive oil
1 small orange-fleshed melon, such as cantaloupe
7 oz/200 g chorizo sausage, outer casing removed
few sprigs of fresh tarragon or flat-leaf parsley, to garnish

dressing
3 tbsp Spanish extra virgin olive oil
1 tbsp red wine vinegar
1 tsp prepared mustard
1 tbsp chopped fresh tarragon
salt and pepper

patatas bravas

**SERVES 6
as part of a tapas meal**

Spanish olive oil, for frying
1 onion, finely chopped
2 garlic cloves, crushed
¼ cup white wine or dry
  Spanish sherry
14 oz/400 g canned chopped
  tomatoes
2 tsp white or red wine vinegar
1–2 tsp crushed dried chiles
2 tsp hot or sweet smoked
  Spanish paprika
2 lb 4 oz/1 kg potatoes
salt

To make the sauce, heat 2 tablespoons of oil in a saucepan, then add the onion and cook over medium heat, stirring occasionally, for 5 minutes, or until softened but not browned. Add the garlic and cook, stirring, for 30 seconds. Add the wine and bring to a boil. Add the tomatoes, vinegar, chiles, and paprika, then reduce the heat and simmer, uncovered, for 10–15 minutes, or until a thick sauce forms.

When the sauce is cooked, use a handheld blender to blend until smooth. Alternatively, transfer the sauce to a food processor and process until smooth. Return the sauce to the pan and set aside.

Do not peel the potatoes, but cut them into chunky pieces. Heat enough oil in a large skillet to come about 1 inch/2.5 cm up the side of the skillet. Add the potato pieces and cook over medium–high heat, turning occasionally, for 10–15 minutes until golden brown. Remove with a slotted spoon and drain on paper towels, then sprinkle with salt.

Meanwhile, gently reheat the sauce. Transfer the potatoes to a warmed serving dish and drizzle over the sauce. Serve hot, with wooden toothpicks to spear the potatoes.

baby potatoes
with aïoli

SERVES 6–8
as part of a tapas meal

1 lb/450 g baby new potatoes
1 tbsp chopped fresh flat-leaf
    parsley
salt

aïoli
1 large egg yolk, at room
    temperature
1 tbsp white wine vinegar or
    lemon juice
2 large garlic cloves, peeled
5 tbsp Spanish extra virgin
    olive oil
5 tbsp corn oil
salt and pepper

To make the aïoli, place the egg yolk, vinegar, garlic, and salt and pepper to taste in a food processor fitted with a metal blade and blend together. With the motor still running, very slowly add the olive oil, then the corn oil, drop by drop at first, then, when it begins to thicken, in a slow, steady stream until the sauce is thick and smooth. Alternatively, use a bowl and whisk to make the aïoli.

For this recipe, the aïoli should be quite thin to coat the potatoes. To ensure this, blend in 1 tablespoon of water to form the consistency of sauce.

To prepare the potatoes, cut them in half or quarters to make bite-size pieces. If they are very small you can leave them whole. Place the potatoes in a large saucepan of cold, lightly salted water and bring to a boil. Reduce the heat and simmer for 7 minutes, or until just tender. Drain well, then transfer to a large bowl.

While the potatoes are still warm, pour over the aïoli sauce and gently toss the potatoes in it. Adding the sauce to the potatoes while they are still warm will help them to absorb the garlic flavor. Let stand for 20 minutes so that the potatoes marinate in the sauce.

Transfer the potatoes with aïoli to a warmed serving dish. Sprinkle over the parsley and salt to taste and serve warm. Alternatively, the dish can be prepared ahead and stored in the refrigerator, but return it to room temperature before serving.

potato wedges with shallots & rosemary

Preheat the oven to 400°F/200°C. Peel and cut each potato into 8 thick wedges. Put the potatoes in a large saucepan of lightly salted water and bring to a boil. Reduce the heat and simmer for 5 minutes.

Heat the oil in a large roasting pan on the stove. Drain the potatoes well and add to the roasting pan. Strip the leaves off the rosemary sprigs, then finely chop and sprinkle over the potatoes.

Roast the potatoes in the preheated oven for 35 minutes, turning twice during cooking. Add the shallots and garlic and roast for an additional 15 minutes, or until golden brown. Season with salt and pepper to taste.

Transfer to a warmed serving dish and serve hot.

SERVES 6
as part of a tapas meal

2 lb 4 oz/1 kg small potatoes
6 tbsp Spanish olive oil
2 fresh rosemary sprigs
5$\frac{1}{2}$ oz/150 g baby shallots
2 garlic cloves, sliced
salt and pepper

meat & poultry

As Spain is a country of serious carnivores, many meat and chicken tapas are popular. The country's seemingly infinite variety of highly prized cured hams and sausages are ideal for tapas in a hurry, as a sandwich filling, or chopped and used to flavor Crispy Chicken & Ham Croquettes.

When you want a tapas that is more than just one bite, take a look at the recipes in this chapter. Moroccan Chicken Kabobs, Beef Skewers with Orange & Garlic, and Lamb Skewers with Lemon are examples of *pinchos*, tapas cooked on small wooden skewers, eliminating the need for knives or forks.

Or try Porterhouse Steak with Garlic & Sherry or Sautéed Chicken with Crispy Garlic Slices.

porterhouse steak
with garlic & sherry

SERVES 6–8
as part of a tapas meal

4 porterhouse steaks, about
   6–8 oz/175–225 g each
   and 1 inch/2.5 cm thick
5 garlic cloves
3 tbsp Spanish olive oil
1/2 cup dry Spanish sherry
salt and pepper
chopped fresh flat-leaf parsley,
   to garnish
crusty bread, to serve

Cut the steaks into 1-inch/2.5-cm cubes and put in a large, shallow dish. Slice 3 of the garlic cloves and set aside. Finely chop the remaining garlic cloves and sprinkle over the steak cubes. Season generously with pepper and mix well together. Cover and let marinate in the refrigerator for 1–2 hours.

Heat the oil in a large skillet, then add the garlic slices and cook over low heat, stirring, for 1 minute, or until golden brown. Increase the heat to medium–high, then add the steak cubes and cook, stirring continuously, for 2–3 minutes, or until browned and almost cooked to your liking.

Add the sherry and cook until it has evaporated slightly. Season with salt to taste and turn into a warmed serving dish. Garnish with chopped parsley and serve hot, accompanied by chunks or slices of crusty bread to mop up the juices.

beef skewers with orange & garlic

SERVES 6–8
as part of a tapas meal

3 tbsp white wine
2 tbsp Spanish olive oil
3 garlic cloves, finely chopped
juice of 1 orange
1 lb/450 g beef top round, cubed
1 lb/450 g pearl onions, halved
2 orange bell peppers, seeded
   and cut into squares
8 oz/225 g cherry tomatoes,
   halved
salt and pepper

Mix the wine, olive oil, garlic, and orange juice together in a shallow, nonmetallic dish. Add the cubes of beef, season with salt and pepper to taste, and toss to coat. Cover with plastic wrap and let marinate in the refrigerator for 2–8 hours.

Preheat the broiler to high. Drain the beef, reserving the marinade. Thread the beef, onions, bell peppers, and tomatoes alternately onto several small skewers.

Cook the skewers under the hot broiler, turning and brushing frequently with the marinade, for 10 minutes, or until cooked through. Transfer to warmed serving plates and serve immediately.

calves' liver in almond saffron sauce

To make the sauce, heat 2 tablespoons of the oil in a large skillet. Tear the bread into small pieces and add to the skillet with the almonds. Cook over low heat, stirring frequently, for 2 minutes, or until golden brown. Stir in the garlic and cook, stirring, for 30 seconds.

Add the saffron and sherry to the skillet and season with salt and pepper to taste. Bring to a boil and continue to boil for 1–2 minutes. Remove from the heat and let cool slightly, then transfer the mixture to a food processor. Add the stock and process until smooth. Set aside.

Cut the liver into large bite-size pieces. Dust lightly with flour and season generously with pepper. Heat the remaining oil in the skillet, then add the liver and cook over medium heat, stirring constantly, for 2–3 minutes, or until firm and lightly browned.

Pour the sauce into the skillet and reheat gently for 1–2 minutes. Transfer to a warmed serving dish and garnish with chopped parsley. Serve hot, accompanied by chunks of crusty bread to mop up the sauce.

**SERVES 6
as part of a tapas meal**

4 tbsp Spanish olive oil
1 oz/25 g white bread
2/3 cup blanched almonds
2 garlic cloves, crushed
pinch of saffron strands
2/3 cup dry Spanish sherry
   or white wine
1 1/4 cups vegetable stock
1 lb/450 g calves' liver
all-purpose flour, for dusting
salt and pepper
chopped fresh flat-leaf parsley,
   to garnish
crusty bread, to serve

lamb skewers
with lemon

SERVES 8
as part of a tapas meal

2 garlic cloves, finely chopped
1 Spanish onion, finely chopped
2 tsp finely grated lemon rind
2 tbsp lemon juice
1 tsp fresh thyme leaves
1 tsp ground coriander
1 tsp ground cumin
2 tbsp red wine vinegar
1/2 cup Spanish olive oil
2 lb 4 oz/1 kg lamb tenderloin,
   cut into 3/4-inch/2-cm pieces
orange or lemon slices,
   to garnish

Mix the garlic, onion, lemon rind, lemon juice, thyme, coriander, cumin, vinegar, and olive oil together in a large, shallow, nonmetallic dish, whisking well until thoroughly combined.

Thread the pieces of lamb on to 16 wooden skewers and add to the dish, turning well to coat. Cover with plastic wrap and let marinate in the refrigerator for 2–8 hours, turning occasionally.

Preheat the broiler to medium. Drain the skewers, reserving the marinade. Cook under the hot broiler, turning frequently and brushing with the marinade, for 10 minutes, or until tender and cooked to your liking.

Serve immediately, garnished with orange or lemon slices.

tiny meatballs
in almond sauce

SERVES 6–8
as part of a tapas meal

2 oz/55 g white or brown bread,
  crusts removed
3 tbsp water
1 lb/450 g fresh ground lean
  pork, beef, or lamb
1 large onion, finely chopped
1 garlic clove, crushed
2 tbsp chopped fresh flat-leaf
  parsley, plus extra to garnish
1 egg, beaten
freshly grated nutmeg
all-purpose flour, for coating
2 tbsp Spanish olive oil
lemon juice, to taste
salt and pepper
crusty bread, to serve

almond sauce
2 tbsp Spanish olive oil
1 oz/25 g white or brown bread
4 oz/115 g blanched almonds
2 garlic cloves, finely chopped
$^2/_3$ cup dry white wine
$1^3/_4$ cups vegetable stock
salt and pepper

To prepare the meatballs, place the bread in a bowl, then add the water and let soak for 5 minutes. With your hands, squeeze out the water and return the bread to a dry bowl. Add the ground meat, onion, garlic, parsley, and egg, then season with grated nutmeg and a little salt and pepper. Knead the ingredients well to form a smooth mixture.

Spread some flour on a plate. With floured hands, shape the meat mixture into about 30 equal-size balls, then roll each meatball again in flour until coated.

Heat the olive oil in a large, heavy-bottom skillet. Add the meatballs, in batches, and cook for 4–5 minutes, or until browned on all sides. Using a slotted spoon, remove the meatballs from the skillet and reserve.

To make the sauce, heat the olive oil in the same skillet in which the meatballs were fried. Break the bread into pieces, then add to the skillet with the almonds and cook gently, stirring frequently, until the bread and almonds are golden brown. Add the garlic and fry for an additional 30 seconds, then pour in the wine and boil for 1–2 minutes. Season with salt and pepper to taste and let cool slightly.

Transfer the almond mixture to a food processor. Pour in the stock and process the mixture until smooth. Return the sauce to the skillet.

Carefully add the meatballs to the almond sauce and simmer for 25 minutes, or until the meatballs are tender. Taste the sauce and season with salt and pepper if necessary.

Transfer the cooked meatballs and sauce to a warmed serving dish, then add a squeeze of lemon juice to taste and sprinkle with chopped parsley to garnish. Serve piping hot with crusty bread for mopping up the almond sauce.

spanish meatballs
with cracked olives

Put the bread in a bowl, then add the water and let soak for 5 minutes. Using your hands, squeeze out as much of the water as possible from the bread and put the bread in a clean bowl.

Add the ground meat, 1 chopped onion, 2 crushed garlic cloves, the cumin, coriander, and egg to the bread. Season with salt to taste and, using your hands, mix together well. Dust a plate or cookie sheet with flour. Using floured hands, roll the mixture into 30 equal-size, small balls, then put on the plate or cookie sheet and roll lightly in the flour.

Heat 2 tablespoons of the oil in a large skillet, then add the meatballs, in batches to avoid overcrowding, and cook over medium heat, turning frequently, for 8–10 minutes, until golden brown on all sides and firm. Remove with a slotted spoon and set aside.

Heat the remaining oil in the skillet, then add the remaining onion and cook, stirring occasionally, for 5 minutes, or until softened but not browned. Add the remaining garlic and cook, stirring, for 30 seconds. Add the tomatoes, sherry, paprika, and sugar and season with salt to taste. Bring to a boil, then reduce the heat and simmer for 10 minutes.

Using a handheld blender, blend the tomato mixture until smooth. Alternatively, turn the tomato mixture into a food processor or blender and process until smooth. Return the sauce to the skillet.

Carefully return the meatballs to the skillet and add the olives. Simmer gently for 20 minutes, or until the meatballs are tender. Serve hot, with crusty bread to mop up the sauce.

SERVES 6
as part of a tapas meal

2 oz/55 g day-old bread, crusts removed
3 tbsp water
$1^1/_8$ cups lean fresh ground pork
$1^1/_8$ cups lean fresh ground lamb
2 small onions, finely chopped
3 garlic cloves, crushed
1 tsp ground cumin
1 tsp ground coriander
1 egg, lightly beaten
all-purpose flour, for dusting
3 tbsp Spanish olive oil
14 oz/400 g canned chopped tomatoes
5 tbsp dry sherry or red wine
pinch of hot or sweet smoked Spanish paprika
pinch of sugar
1 cup cracked green Spanish olives in extra virgin olive oil
salt
crusty bread, to serve

spareribs coated in paprika sauce

SERVES 6
as part of a tapas meal

Spanish olive oil, for oiling
2 lb 12 oz/1.25 kg pork
    spareribs
1/3 cup dry Spanish sherry
5 tsp hot or sweet smoked
    Spanish paprika
2 garlic cloves, crushed
1 tbsp dried oregano
2/3 cup water
salt

Preheat the oven to 425°F/220°C. Oil a large roasting pan. If the butcher has not already done so, cut the sheets of spareribs into individual ribs. If possible, cut each sparerib in half widthwise. Put the spareribs in the prepared pan, in a single layer, and roast in the preheated oven for 20 minutes.

Meanwhile, make the sauce. Put the sherry, paprika, garlic, oregano, water, and salt to taste in a pitcher and mix together well.

Reduce the oven temperature to 350°F/180°C. Pour off the fat from the pan, then pour the sauce over the spareribs and turn them to coat with the sauce on both sides. Roast for an additional 45 minutes, basting with the sauce once halfway through the cooking time, until tender.

Pile the spareribs into a warmed serving dish. Bring the sauce in the pan to a boil on the stove, then reduce the heat and simmer until reduced by half. Pour the sauce over the spareribs and serve hot.

miniature pork brochettes

SERVES 4–6
as part of a tapas meal

1 lb/450 g lean, boneless pork
3 tbsp Spanish olive oil,
   plus extra for oiling (optional)
grated rind and juice of
   1 large lemon
2 garlic cloves, crushed
2 tbsp chopped fresh flat-leaf
   parsley, plus extra to garnish
1 tbsp ras-el-hanout spice blend
salt and pepper

The brochettes are marinated overnight, so remember to do this in advance so that they are ready when you need them. Cut the pork into pieces about 3/4 inch/2 cm square and put in a large, shallow, nonmetallic dish that will hold the pieces in a single layer.

To prepare the marinade, place all the remaining ingredients in a bowl and mix together. Pour the marinade over the pork and toss the meat in it until well coated. Cover the dish and let marinate in the refrigerator for 8 hours or overnight, stirring the pork 2–3 times.

You can use wooden or metal skewers to cook the brochettes and for this recipe you will need about 12 x 6-inch/15-cm skewers. If you are using wooden ones, soak them in cold water for 30 minutes prior to using. Metal skewers simply need to be greased.

Preheat the broiler or grill pan. Thread 3 marinated pork pieces, leaving a little space between each piece, on to each prepared skewer. Cook the brochettes for 10–15 minutes, or until tender and lightly charred, turning several times and basting with the remaining marinade during cooking. Serve the pork brochettes piping hot, garnished with parsley.

serrano ham croquettes

Heat the olive oil in a saucepan, then add the onion and cook over medium heat, stirring occasionally, for 5 minutes, or until softened but not browned. Add the garlic and cook, stirring, for 30 seconds. Stir in the flour and cook over low heat, stirring continuously, for 1 minute, without the mixture coloring.

Remove the pan from the heat and gradually stir in the milk to form a smooth sauce. Return to the heat and slowly bring to a boil, stirring continuously, until the sauce boils and thickens.

Remove the pan from the heat, then stir in the ham and paprika and season with salt to taste. Spread the mixture in a shallow dish and let cool, then cover and chill in the refrigerator for at least 2 hours or overnight.

When the mixture has chilled, break the egg onto a plate and beat lightly. Spread the breadcrumbs on a separate plate. Using wet hands, form the ham mixture into 8 even-size pieces and form each piece into a cylindrical shape. Dip the croquettes, one at a time, into the beaten egg, then roll in the breadcrumbs to coat. Put on a plate and chill in the refrigerator for at least 1 hour.

Heat enough sunflower oil for deep-frying in a deep-fat fryer to 350–375°F/180–190°C, or until a cube of bread browns in 30 seconds. Add the croquettes, in batches to avoid overcrowding, and cook for 5 minutes, or until golden brown and crisp. Remove with a slotted spoon or draining basket and drain on paper towels. Keep hot in a warm oven while you cook the remaining croquettes. Serve hot with aïoli.

SERVES 4
as part of a tapas meal

4 tbsp Spanish olive oil
1 small onion, finely chopped
1 garlic clove, crushed
4 tbsp all-purpose flour
scant 1 cup milk
7 oz/200 g serrano ham or
    cooked ham, in one piece,
    finely diced
pinch of hot or sweet smoked
    Spanish paprika
1 egg
1 cup day-old white
    breadcrumbs
sunflower oil, for deep-frying
salt
Aïoli (see page 58), to serve

roasted asparagus with mountain ham

SERVES 4–6
as part of a tapas meal

2 tbsp Spanish olive oil
6 slices serrano ham
12 asparagus spears
pepper
Aïoli (see page 58), to serve

Preheat the oven to 400°F/200°C. Put half the olive oil in a roasting pan that will hold the asparagus spears in a single layer and swirl it around so that it covers the bottom. Cut each slice of serrano ham in half lengthwise.

Trim the ends of the asparagus spears, then wrap a slice of ham round the stem end of each spear. Place the wrapped spears in the prepared roasting pan and lightly brush the ham and asparagus with the remaining olive oil. Season the spears with pepper.

Roast the asparagus spears in the oven for 10 minutes, depending on the thickness of the asparagus, or until tender but still firm. Do not overcook the asparagus spears as it is important that they are still firm.

Serve piping hot, accompanied by a bowl of aïoli for dipping.

empanadillas with ham & goat cheese

**SERVES 16
as part of a tapas meal**

1 tbsp Spanish olive oil
1 small onion, finely chopped
1 garlic clove, crushed
5¹/₂ oz/150 g soft goat cheese
6 oz/175 g thickly sliced cooked
   ham, finely chopped
scant ¹/₂ cup capers, chopped
¹/₂ tsp hot or sweet smoked
   Spanish paprika
1 lb 2 oz/500 g prepared puff
   pastry, thawed if frozen
all-purpose flour, for dusting
beaten egg, for glazing
salt

Preheat the oven to 400°F/200°C. Dampen several large cookie sheets. Heat the oil in a large skillet, then add the onion and cook over medium heat, stirring occasionally, for 5 minutes, or until softened but not browned. Add the garlic and cook, stirring, for 30 seconds.

Put the goat cheese in a bowl, then add the ham, capers, onion mixture, and paprika and mix together well. Season with salt to taste.

Thinly roll out the pastry on a lightly floured counter. Using a plain, 3¹/₄-inch/8-cm round cutter, cut out 32 circles, rerolling the trimmings as necessary. Using a teaspoon, put an equal, small amount of the goat cheese mixture in the center of each pastry circle. Dampen the edges of the pastry with a little water and fold one half over the other to form a crescent and enclose the filling. Pinch the edges together with your fingers to seal, then press with the tines of a fork to seal more securely. Transfer to the prepared cookie sheets.

With the tip of a sharp knife, make a small slit in the top of each pastry and brush with beaten egg to glaze. Bake in the preheated oven for 15 minutes, or until risen and golden brown. Serve warm.

chorizo in red wine

Before you begin, bear in mind that this dish is best if prepared the day before you are planning to serve it. Using a fork, prick the chorizo in 3 or 4 places. Place the chorizo and wine in a large saucepan. Bring the wine to a boil, then reduce the heat and simmer gently, covered, for 15–20 minutes. Transfer the chorizo and wine to a bowl or dish, cover, and let the sausage marinate in the wine for 8 hours or overnight.

The next day, remove the chorizo from the bowl or dish and reserve the wine. Remove the outer casing from the chorizo and cut the sausage into 1/4-inch/5-mm slices. Place the slices in a large, heavy-bottom skillet or flameproof serving dish.

If you are adding the brandy, pour it into a small saucepan and heat gently. Pour the brandy over the chorizo slices, then stand well back and set aflame. When the flames have died down, shake the pan gently and add the reserved wine, then cook over high heat until almost all of the wine has evaporated.

Serve the chorizo in red wine piping hot, in the dish in which it was cooked, sprinkled with parsley to garnish. Accompany with chunks or slices of bread to mop up the juices and provide wooden toothpicks to spear the pieces of chorizo.

SERVES 6
as part of a tapas meal

7 oz/200 g chorizo sausage
3/4 cup Spanish red wine
2 tbsp brandy (optional)
chopped fresh flat-leaf parsley, to garnish
crusty bread, to serve

fried chorizo with herbs

SERVES 6–8
as part of a tapas meal

1 lb 9 oz/700 g chorizo cooking
  sausage
2 tbsp olive oil
2 garlic cloves, finely chopped
4 tbsp chopped mixed fresh
  herbs

Using a sharp knife, cut the chorizo into $1/4$-inch/5-mm thick slices. Heat a large, heavy-bottom skillet. Add the chorizo slices, without any additional fat, and cook over medium heat, stirring frequently, for 5 minutes, or until crisp and browned.

  Remove the chorizo slices with a spatula or slotted spoon and drain well on paper towels. Drain the fat from the skillet and wipe out with a pad of paper towels.

  Heat the olive oil in the skillet over a medium–low heat. Add the chorizo slices, garlic, and herbs and cook, stirring occasionally, until heated through. Serve immediately.

chickpeas & chorizo

SERVES 4–6
as part of a tapas meal

9 oz/250 g chorizo sausage in
    1 piece, outer casing removed
4 tbsp Spanish olive oil
1 onion, finely chopped
1 large garlic clove, crushed
14 oz/400 g canned chickpeas,
    drained and rinsed
6 pimientos del piquillo, drained,
    patted dry, and sliced
1 tbsp sherry vinegar, or to taste
salt and pepper
finely chopped fresh parsley,
    to garnish
crusty bread slices, to serve

Cut the chorizo into $^1/_2$-inch/1-cm dice. Heat the oil in a heavy-bottom skillet over medium heat, then add the onion and garlic. Cook, stirring occasionally, until the onion is softened but not browned. Stir in the chorizo and cook until heated through.

Transfer the mixture to a bowl and stir in the chickpeas and pimientos. Splash with sherry vinegar and season with salt and pepper to taste. Serve hot or at room temperature, generously sprinkled with parsley, with plenty of crusty bread.

chorizo & mushroom kabobs

Heat the oil in a skillet over medium heat. Add the chorizo and cook for 20 seconds, stirring.

Add the mushrooms and continue cooking for an additional 1–2 minutes until the mushrooms begin to brown and absorb the fat in the skillet.

Thread a bell pepper square, a piece of chorizo, and a mushroom on to a wooden toothpick. Continue until all the ingredients are used. Serve hot or at room temperature.

SERVES 8
as part of a tapas meal

2 tbsp Spanish olive oil
24 slices chorizo sausage, each
  about 1/2 inch/1 cm thick
  (about 3 1/2 oz/100 g)
24 button mushrooms, wiped
1 green bell pepper, roasted,
  peeled, and cut into
  24 squares

crispy chicken
& ham croquettes

SERVES 4
as part of a tapas meal

4 tbsp Spanish olive oil or
    butter
4 tbsp all-purpose flour
3/4 cup milk
4 oz/115 g cooked chicken,
    ground
2 oz/55 g serrano or cooked
    ham, very finely chopped
1 tbsp chopped fresh flat-leaf
    parsley
small pinch of freshly grated
    nutmeg
1 egg, beaten
1 cup day-old white
    breadcrumbs
corn oil, for deep-frying
salt and pepper
Aïoli (see page 58), to serve

Heat the oil in a saucepan. Stir in the flour to form a paste and cook gently for 1 minute, stirring continuously. Remove the pan from the heat and gradually stir in the milk until smooth. Return to the heat and slowly bring to a boil, stirring continuously, until the mixture thickens.

Remove the pan from the heat, add the chicken and beat until the mixture is smooth. Add the ham, parsley, and nutmeg and mix well. Season the mixture with salt and pepper to taste. Spread the chicken mixture in a dish and let stand for 30 minutes until cool, then cover and let chill for 2–3 hours or overnight. Don't be tempted to skip this stage, as chilling the croquettes helps to prevent them from falling apart when they are cooked.

When the chicken mixture has chilled, pour the beaten egg onto a plate and spread out the breadcrumbs on a separate plate. Divide the chicken mixture into 8 equal-size portions. With dampened hands, form each portion into a cylindrical shape. Dip the croquettes, one at a time, in the beaten egg, then roll in the breadcrumbs to coat them. Place on a plate and let chill for 1 hour.

To cook, heat the corn oil in a deep-fat fryer to 350–375°F/180–190°C, or until a cube of bread browns in 30 seconds. Add the croquettes, in batches to prevent the temperature of the oil from dropping, and deep-fry for 5–10 minutes, or until golden brown and crispy. Remove with a slotted spoon and drain well on paper towels.

Serve the chicken and ham croquettes piping hot, accompanied by a bowl of aïoli for dipping.

sautéed chicken
with crispy garlic slices

SERVES 8
as part of a tapas meal

8 skin-on chicken thighs,
   boned if available
hot or sweet smoked Spanish
   paprika, to taste
4 tbsp Spanish olive oil
10 garlic cloves, sliced
1/2 cup dry white wine
1 bay leaf
salt
chopped fresh flat-leaf parsley,
   to garnish
crusty bread, to serve (optional)

If necessary, halve the chicken thighs and remove the bones, then cut the flesh into bite-size pieces, leaving the skin on. Season with paprika to taste.

Heat the oil in a large skillet or an ovenproof casserole, then add the garlic slices and cook over medium heat, stirring frequently, for 1 minute, or until golden brown. Remove with a slotted spoon and drain on paper towels.

Add the chicken thighs to the skillet and cook, turning occasionally, for 10 minutes, or until tender and golden brown on all sides. Add the wine and bay leaf and bring to a boil. Reduce the heat and simmer, stirring occasionally, for 10 minutes, or until most of the liquid has evaporated and the juices run clear when a skewer is inserted into the thickest part of the meat. Season with salt to taste.

Transfer the chicken to a warmed serving dish and sprinkle over the reserved garlic slices. Sprinkle with chopped parsley to garnish and serve with chunks of crusty bread to mop up the juices, if using.

chicken rolls with olives

Preheat the oven to 400°F/200°C. Pit and finely chop the olives. Mix the olives, butter, and parsley together in a bowl.

Place the chicken breasts between 2 sheets of plastic wrap and beat gently with a meat mallet or the side of a rolling pin.

Spread the olive and herb butter over one side of each flattened chicken breast and roll up. Secure with a wooden toothpick or tie with clean string if necessary.

Place the chicken rolls in an ovenproof dish. Drizzle over the oil from the olive jar and bake in the preheated oven for 45–55 minutes, or until tender and the juices run clear when the chicken is pierced with the point of a sharp knife.

Transfer the chicken rolls to a cutting board and discard the toothpicks. Using a sharp knife, cut into slices, then transfer to warmed serving plates and serve.

SERVES 6–8
as part of a tapas meal

$2/3$ cup black Spanish olives in oil, drained, and 2 tbsp oil reserved
$2/3$ cup butter, softened
4 tbsp chopped fresh parsley
4 skinless, boneless chicken breasts

moroccan chicken kabobs

SERVES 4
as part of a tapas meal

1 lb/450 g chicken breast fillets
3 tbsp Spanish olive oil,
   plus extra for oiling
juice of 1 lemon
2 garlic cloves, crushed
1½ tsp ground cumin
1 tsp ground coriander
1 tsp hot or sweet smoked
   Spanish paprika
¼ tsp ground cinnamon
½ tsp dried oregano
salt
chopped fresh flat-leaf parsley,
   to garnish

Cut the chicken into 1-inch/2.5-cm cubes and put in a large, shallow, nonmetallic dish. Put all the remaining ingredients, except the parsley, in a bowl and whisk together. Pour the marinade over the chicken cubes and toss the meat in the marinade until well coated. Cover and let marinate in the refrigerator for 8 hours or overnight, turning the chicken 2–3 times if possible.

If using wooden skewers, soak the skewers in cold water for about 30 minutes to help prevent them from burning and the food sticking to them during cooking. If using metal skewers, lightly brush with oil. Preheat the broiler or grill pan. Remove the chicken pieces from the marinade, reserving the remaining marinade, and thread an equal quantity on to each prepared skewer, leaving a little space between each piece.

Brush the broiler rack or grill pan with a little oil. Add the kabobs and cook, turning frequently and brushing with the reserved marinade halfway through cooking, for 15 minutes, or until browned on all sides, tender, and cooked through. Serve hot, sprinkled with chopped parsley to garnish.

chicken wings
with tomato dressing

SERVES 6–8
as part of a tapas meal

3/4 cup Spanish olive oil
3 garlic cloves, finely chopped
1 tsp ground cumin
2 lb 4 oz/1 kg chicken wings
2 tomatoes, peeled, seeded,
    and diced
5 tbsp white wine vinegar
1 tbsp shredded fresh basil
    leaves

Preheat the oven to 350°F/180°C. Mix 1 tablespoon of the oil with the garlic and cumin in a shallow dish. Cut off and discard the tips of the chicken wings and add the wings to the spice mixture, turning to coat. Cover with plastic wrap and let marinate in a cool place for 15 minutes.

Heat 3 tablespoons of the remaining oil in a large, heavy-bottom skillet. Add the chicken wings, in batches, and cook, turning frequently, until golden brown. Transfer to a roasting pan.

Roast the chicken wings for 10–15 minutes, or until tender and the juices run clear when the point of a sharp knife is inserted into the thickest part of the meat.

Meanwhile, mix the remaining olive oil, the tomatoes, vinegar, and basil together in a bowl.

Using tongs, transfer the chicken wings to a nonmetallic dish. Pour the dressing over them, turning to coat. Cover with plastic wrap and let cool, then chill for 4 hours. Remove from the refrigerator 30–60 minutes before serving to return to room temperature.

chicken livers in sherry sauce

If necessary, trim the livers, cutting away any ducts and gristle, then cut into small, bite-size pieces. Heat the oil in a large, heavy-bottom skillet. Add the onion and cook for 5 minutes, or until softened but not browned. Add the garlic and cook for an additional 30 seconds.

Add the livers to the skillet and cook for 2–3 minutes, stirring continuously, until they are firm and have changed color on the outside but are still pink and soft in the center. Using a slotted spoon, lift the livers from the skillet and transfer to a large, warmed serving dish or several smaller ones. Keep warm.

Add the sherry to the skillet, increase the heat, and let it bubble for 3–4 minutes to evaporate the alcohol and reduce slightly. At the same time, deglaze the skillet by scraping and stirring all the bits on the bottom of the skillet into the sauce with a wooden spoon. Season the sauce with salt and pepper to taste.

Pour the sherry sauce over the chicken livers and sprinkle over the parsley. Garnish with parsley sprigs and serve piping hot with chunks or slices of crusty bread or toast to mop up the sauce.

SERVES 6
as part of a tapas meal

1 lb/450 g chicken livers
2 tbsp Spanish olive oil
1 small onion, finely chopped
2 garlic cloves, finely chopped
scant $1/2$ cup dry Spanish sherry
2 tbsp chopped fresh flat-leaf
 parsley, plus extra sprigs
 to garnish
salt and pepper
crusty bread or toast,
 to serve

chicken salad
with raisins & pine nuts

SERVES 6–8
as part of a tapas meal

1/4 cup red wine vinegar
1/8 cup superfine sugar
1 bay leaf
pared rind of 1 lemon
scant 1 cup seedless raisins
4 large skinless, boneless
  chicken breasts, about
  1 lb 5 oz/600 g in total
5 tbsp Spanish olive oil
1 garlic clove, finely chopped
1 cup pine nuts
1/3 cup Spanish extra virgin
  olive oil
1 small bunch of fresh flat-leaf
  parsley, finely chopped
salt and pepper

To make the dressing, put the vinegar, sugar, bay leaf, and lemon rind in a saucepan and bring to a boil, then remove from the heat. Stir in the raisins and let cool.

When the dressing is cool, slice the chicken breasts widthwise into very thin slices. Heat the olive oil in a large skillet, then add the chicken slices and cook over medium heat, stirring occasionally, for 8–10 minutes, or until lightly browned and tender.

Add the garlic and pine nuts and cook, stirring continuously and shaking the skillet, for 1 minute, or until the pine nuts are golden brown. Season with salt and pepper to taste.

Pour the cooled dressing into a large bowl, discarding the bay leaf and lemon rind. Add the extra virgin olive oil and whisk together. Season with salt and pepper to taste. Add the chicken mixture and parsley and toss together. Turn the salad into a serving dish and serve warm or, if serving cold, cover and chill in the refrigerator for 2–3 hours before serving.

chicken in lemon
& garlic

SERVES 6–8
as part of a tapas meal

4 large skinless, boneless
   chicken breasts
5 tbsp Spanish olive oil
1 onion, finely chopped
6 garlic cloves, finely chopped
grated rind of 1 lemon, finely
   pared rind of 1 lemon, and
   juice of both lemons
4 tbsp chopped fresh flat-leaf
   parsley, plus extra to garnish
salt and pepper
lemon wedges and crusty
   bread, to serve

Using a sharp knife, slice the chicken breasts widthwise into very thin slices. Heat the olive oil in a large, heavy-bottom skillet, add the onion and cook for 5 minutes, or until softened but not browned. Add the garlic and cook for an additional 30 seconds.

Add the sliced chicken to the skillet and cook gently for 5–10 minutes, stirring occasionally, until all the ingredients are lightly browned and the chicken is tender.

Add the grated lemon rind and the lemon juice and let it bubble. At the same time, deglaze the skillet by scraping and stirring all the bits on the bottom of the skillet into the juices with a wooden spoon. Remove the skillet from the heat, stir in the parsley, and season with salt and pepper to taste.

Transfer the chicken in lemon and garlic, piping hot, to a warmed serving dish. Sprinkle with the pared lemon rind, garnish with the parsley, and serve with lemon wedges for squeezing over the chicken, accompanied by chunks or slices of crusty bread for mopping up the lemon and garlic juices.

fish & seafood

With miles of coastline along the Atlantic Ocean and Mediterranean, Spanish fishermen provide cooks with a wealth of fresh fish and shellfish, which results in wonderful seafood tapas, sometimes as simple as peeled shrimp on toothpicks.

Yet even with such fresh choices, Spaniards still love salt cod, often the only seafood available in the days before modern transportation, and Salt Cod Fritters with Spinach are always popular.

This chapter contains recipes from all over the country, and land and sea come together in Scallops with Serrano Ham and Rosemary Skewers with Monkfish & Bacon. In the sunny south, Sizzling Chili Shrimp is the ubiquitous tapas.

salt cod fritters
with spinach

SERVES 16
as part of a tapas meal

9 oz/250 g dried salt cod in
   1 piece
1 cup all-purpose flour
1 tsp baking powder
1/4 tsp salt
1 large egg, lightly beaten
about 2/3 cup milk
2 lemon slices
2 fresh parsley sprigs
1 bay leaf
1/2 tbsp garlic-flavored olive oil
3 oz/85 g fresh baby spinach,
   rinsed
1/4 tsp smoked sweet, mild, or
   hot Spanish paprika, to taste
Spanish olive oil, for frying
coarse sea salt (optional)
Aïoli (see page 58), to serve

Place the dried salt cod in a large bowl. Cover with cold water and let soak for 48 hours, changing the water at least 3 times a day.

Meanwhile, make the batter. Sift the flour, baking powder, and salt into a large bowl and make a well. Mix the egg with 1/2 cup of the milk and pour into the well in the flour, stirring to make a smooth batter with a thick coating consistency. If it seems too thick, gradually stir in the remaining milk, then let stand for at least 1 hour.

After the salt cod has soaked, transfer it to a large skillet. Add the lemon slices, parsley sprigs, bay leaf, and enough water to cover and bring to a boil. Reduce the heat and simmer for 30–45 minutes, or until the fish is tender and flakes easily.

Meanwhile, prepare the spinach. Heat the garlic-flavored olive oil in a small saucepan over medium heat. Add the spinach with just the water clinging to the leaves and cook for 3–4 minutes, or until wilted.

Drain the spinach in a strainer, using the back of a spoon to press out any excess moisture. Finely chop the spinach, then stir it into the batter with the paprika.

Remove the fish from the water and flake the flesh into pieces, removing all the skin and tiny bones. Stir the flesh into the batter.

Heat 2 inches/5 cm of oil in a heavy-bottom skillet to 350–375°F/ 180–190°C, or until a cube of bread browns in 30 seconds. Use a greased tablespoon or measuring spoon to drop spoonfuls of the batter into the oil, then cook for 8–10 minutes, or until golden brown. Work in batches to avoid crowding the skillet. Use a slotted spoon to transfer the fritters to paper towels to drain and sprinkle with sea salt, if using.

Serve hot or at room temperature with aïoli for dipping.

cod & caper croquettes

SERVES 4–6
as part of a tapas meal

12 oz/350 g white fish fillets,
    such as cod, haddock, or
    monkfish
1¼ cups milk
4 tbsp olive oil or 2 oz/55 g
    butter
scant ½ cup all-purpose flour
4 tbsp capers, coarsely chopped
1 tsp paprika
1 garlic clove, crushed
1 tsp lemon juice
3 tbsp chopped fresh flat-leaf
    parsley, plus extra sprigs
    to garnish
1 egg, beaten
1 cup fresh white breadcrumbs
1 tbsp sesame seeds
corn oil, for deep-frying
salt and pepper
lemon wedges, to garnish
mayonnaise, to serve

Put the fish fillets in a large, heavy-bottom skillet. Pour in the milk and season with salt and pepper to taste. Bring to a boil, then reduce the heat, cover the skillet, and let simmer gently for 8–10 minutes, or until the fish flakes easily when tested with a fork. Using a spatula, remove the fish fillets from the skillet. Pour the milk into a pitcher and set aside for later. Flake the fish, removing and discarding the skin and bones.

Heat the olive oil in a saucepan. Stir in the flour to form a paste and cook gently, stirring, for 1 minute. Remove the pan from the heat and gradually stir in the reserved milk until smooth. Return to the heat and slowly bring to a boil, stirring all the time, until the mixture thickens.

Remove the pan from the heat, add the flaked fish, and beat until the mixture is smooth. Add the capers, paprika, garlic, lemon juice, and parsley and mix well together. Season the mixture with salt and pepper to taste. Spread the fish mixture in a dish and let stand until cool, then cover and put in the refrigerator for 2–3 hours or overnight.

When the fish mixture has chilled, pour the beaten egg onto a plate. Put the breadcrumbs and sesame seeds on a separate plate, mix together, and spread out. Divide the fish mixture into 12 equal-size portions. Then, with lightly floured hands, form each portion into a sausage shape, measuring about 3 inches/7.5 cm in length. Dip the croquettes, one at a time, in the beaten egg, and roll in the breadcrumb mixture to coat them. Place on a plate and let chill for about 1 hour.

To cook the croquettes, heat the oil in a deep-fat fryer to 350–375°F/ 180–190°C, or until a cube of bread browns in 30 seconds. Add the croquettes, in batches, and deep-fry for 3 minutes, or until golden brown and crispy. Remove with a slotted spoon and drain well on paper towels.

Serve piping hot, garnished with lemon wedges and parsley sprigs, and accompanied by a bowl of mayonnaise for dipping.

sardines with romesco sauce

First make the sauce. Preheat the oven to 425°F/220°C. Place the bell pepper, tomatoes, and garlic in an ovenproof dish and drizzle over 1 tablespoon of the oil, turning to coat. Bake in the preheated oven for 20–25 minutes, then remove from the oven and let cool. When cool enough to handle, peel off the skins and place the flesh in a food processor.

Heat 1 tablespoon of the remaining oil in a skillet. Add the bread and almonds and cook over low heat for a few minutes until browned. Remove and drain on paper towels. Add the chile, shallots, and paprika to the skillet and cook for 5 minutes, or until the shallots are softened.

Transfer the almond mixture and shallot mixture to a food processor and add the vinegar, sugar, and water. Process to a paste. With the motor still running, gradually add the remaining oil through the feeder tube. Transfer to a bowl, cover, and reserve.

Place the sardines, skin-side up, on a cutting board and press along the length of the spines with your thumbs. Turn over and remove and discard the bones. Place the flour and eggs in separate bowls. Mix the breadcrumbs and herbs together in a third bowl. Toss the fish in the flour, the eggs, and then in the breadcrumbs.

Heat the vegetable oil in a large saucepan to 350–375°F/180–190°C, or until a cube of bread browns in 30 seconds. Deep-fry the fish for 4–5 minutes, or until golden and tender. Drain and serve with the sauce.

SERVES 6
as part of a tapas meal

24 fresh sardines, scaled, cleaned, and heads removed
heaping 3/4 cup all-purpose flour
4 eggs, lightly beaten
9 oz/250 g fresh white breadcrumbs
6 tbsp chopped fresh parsley
4 tbsp chopped fresh marjoram
vegetable oil, for deep-frying

romesco sauce
1 red bell pepper, halved and seeded
2 tomatoes, halved
4 garlic cloves
1/2 cup Spanish olive oil
1 slice white bread, diced
4 tbsp blanched almonds
1 fresh red chile, seeded and chopped
2 shallots, chopped
1 tsp paprika
2 tbsp red wine vinegar
2 tsp sugar
1 tbsp water

fresh salmon with red bell pepper sauce

SERVES 6
as part of a tapas meal

2 red bell peppers
about 4 tbsp Spanish olive oil
1 lb 9 oz/700 g salmon fillets
1 onion, coarsely chopped
1 garlic clove, finely chopped
6 tbsp dry white wine
1/3 cup heavy cream
salt and pepper
chopped fresh flat-leaf parsley,
   to garnish
crusty bread, to serve (optional)

Preheat the oven to 400°F/200°C. Brush the red bell peppers with 2 teaspoons of the oil and put in a roasting pan. Roast in the preheated oven for 30 minutes, then turn over and roast for an additional 10 minutes, or until the skins have blistered and blackened.

Meanwhile, remove the skin from the salmon fillets and cut the flesh into 1-inch/2.5-cm cubes. Season with pepper to taste and set aside.

Heat 2 tablespoons of the remaining oil in a large skillet, then add the onion and cook, stirring occasionally, for 5 minutes, or until softened but not browned. Add the garlic and cook, stirring, for 30 seconds, or until softened. Add the wine and bring to a boil, then let bubble for 1 minute. Remove from the heat and set aside.

When the bell peppers are cooked, transfer to a plastic bag, using a slotted spoon, and let stand for 15 minutes, or until cool enough to handle. Using a sharp knife or your fingers, carefully peel away the skin from the bell peppers. Halve the bell peppers and remove the stems, cores, and seeds, then put the flesh in a food processor.

Add the onion mixture and cream to the bell peppers and process to a smooth puree. Season with salt and pepper to taste and pour into a saucepan.

Heat the remaining oil in the skillet, then add the salmon cubes and cook, turning occasionally, for 8–10 minutes, or until cooked through and golden brown on both sides. Meanwhile, gently heat the sauce in the pan.

Transfer the cooked salmon to a warmed serving dish. Drizzle over some of the bell pepper sauce and serve the remaining sauce in a small serving bowl. Serve hot, garnished with chopped parsley and accompanied by crusty bread to mop up the sauce, if using.

rosemary skewers
with monkfish & bacon

SERVES 12
as part of a tapas meal

12 oz/350 g monkfish tail or
   9 oz/250 g monkfish fillet
12 fresh rosemary stems
3 tbsp Spanish olive oil
juice of ¹/₂ small lemon
1 garlic clove, crushed
6 thick strips Canadian bacon
salt and pepper
lemon wedges, to garnish
Aïoli (see page 58), to serve

If using monkfish tail, cut either side of the central bone with a sharp knife and remove the flesh to form 2 fillets. Slice the fillets in half lengthwise, then cut each fillet into 12 bite-size chunks to give a total of 24 pieces. Place the monkfish pieces in a large bowl.

To prepare the rosemary skewers, strip the leaves off the stems and reserve them, leaving a few leaves at one end. For the marinade, finely chop the reserved leaves and whisk together in a bowl with the olive oil, lemon juice, garlic, and salt and pepper to taste. Add the monkfish pieces and toss until coated in the marinade. Cover and let marinate in the refrigerator for 1–2 hours.

Cut each bacon strip in half lengthwise, then in half widthwise, and roll up each piece. Thread 2 pieces of monkfish alternately with 2 bacon rolls on to each of the prepared rosemary skewers.

Preheat the broiler. Broil the skewers for 10 minutes, turning occasionally and basting with any remaining marinade, or until cooked. Serve hot, garnished with lemon wedges for squeezing over them and accompanied by a small bowl of aïoli in which to dip the monkfish skewers.

mixed seafood kabobs
with a chili & lime glaze

Pull off the heads of the shrimp. With your fingers, peel away the shells, leaving the tails intact. Using a sharp knife, make a shallow slit along the length of the back of each shrimp, then use the tip of the knife to lift out the dark vein and discard. Rinse the shrimp under cold running water and pat dry with paper towels. Cut the monkfish and salmon into 1-inch/2.5-cm pieces.

Grate the ginger into a strainer set over a large, nonmetallic bowl to catch the juice. Squeeze the grated ginger to extract all the juice and discard the pulp.

Add the chili sauce and lime rind and juice to the ginger juice and mix together. Add the prepared seafood and stir to coat in the marinade. Cover and let marinate in the refrigerator for 30 minutes.

Meanwhile, if using wooden skewers, soak 8 in cold water for about 30 minutes to help prevent them from burning and the food from sticking to them during cooking. If using metal skewers, lightly brush with oil.

Preheat the broiler to high and line the broiler pan with foil. Remove the seafood from the marinade, reserving the remaining marinade, and thread an equal quantity on to each prepared skewer, leaving a little space between each piece. Arrange in the broiler pan.

Cook the skewers under the broiler, turning once and brushing with the reserved marinade, for 6–8 minutes, or until cooked through. Serve hot, drizzled with the marinade in the broiler pan and with lime wedges for squeezing over.

SERVES 4
as part of a tapas meal

16 raw jumbo shrimp, in their shells
12 oz/350 g monkfish or hake fillet
12 oz/350 g salmon fillet, skinned
1-inch/2.5-cm piece fresh ginger
4 tbsp sweet chili sauce
grated rind and juice of 1 lime
sunflower or Spanish olive oil, for oiling (optional)
lime wedges, to serve

batter-fried fish sticks

SERVES 6
as part of a tapas meal

heaping 3/4 cup all-purpose
   flour, plus extra for dusting
pinch of salt
1 egg, beaten
1 tbsp Spanish olive oil
2/3 cup water
1 lb 5 oz/600 g firm-fleshed
   white fish fillet, such as
   monkfish or hake
sunflower or Spanish olive oil,
   for deep-frying
lemon wedges, to serve

To make the batter, put the flour and salt into a large bowl and make a well in the center. Pour the egg and the olive oil into the well, then gradually add the water, mixing in the flour from the side and beating constantly, until all the flour is incorporated and a smooth batter forms.

Cut the fish into sticks about 3/4 inch/2 cm wide and 2 inches/5 cm long. Dust lightly with flour so that the batter sticks to them when dipped in it.

Heat enough sunflower oil for deep-frying in a deep-fat fryer to 350–375°F/180–190°C, or until a cube of bread browns in 30 seconds. Spear a fish stick onto a toothpick and dip into the batter, then drop the fish and toothpick into the hot oil. Cook the fish sticks, in batches to avoid overcrowding, for 5 minutes, or until golden brown. Remove with a slotted spoon or draining basket and drain on paper towels. Keep hot in a warm oven while cooking the remaining fish sticks.

Serve the fish sticks hot, with lemon wedges for squeezing over.

tuna-stuffed bell pepper strips

SERVES 8
as part of a tapas meal

6 mixed red, green, yellow,
   or orange bell peppers
2 tbsp Spanish olive oil
7 oz/200 g canned tuna in olive
   oil, drained
scant 1/2 cup curd cheese
4 tbsp chopped fresh flat-leaf
   parsley
1 garlic clove, crushed
salt and pepper

Preheat the oven to 400°F/200°C. Brush the bell peppers with the oil and put in a roasting pan. Roast in the preheated oven for 30 minutes, then turn over and roast for an additional 10 minutes, or until the skins have blistered and blackened.

Using a slotted spoon, transfer the roasted peppers to a plastic bag and let cool for about 15 minutes, or until cool enough to handle.

Meanwhile, put the tuna on paper towels and pat dry to remove the oil. Transfer to a food processor, then add the curd cheese, parsley, and garlic and process until mixed together. Season with salt and pepper to taste. Using a sharp knife or your fingers, carefully peel away the skins from the cooled bell peppers. Cut the bell peppers into quarters and remove the stems, cores, and seeds.

Put a heaping teaspoonful of the tuna and cheese mixture on the pointed end of each bell pepper quarter and roll up. If necessary, wipe with paper towels to remove any filling that has spread over the skins, then arrange the rolls in a shallow dish with the filling end facing up. Cover and let chill in the refrigerator for at least 2 hours, or until firm, before serving.

empanadillas with tuna & olives

Drain the tuna, reserving the oil, put in a large bowl, and set aside. Heat 1 tablespoon of the reserved oil from the tuna in a large skillet, then add the onion and cook over medium heat, stirring occasionally, for 5 minutes, or until softened but not browned. Add the garlic and cook, stirring, for 30 seconds, or until softened.

Mash the tuna with a fork, then add the onion mixture, olives, and pine nuts and mix together well. Season with salt and pepper to taste.

Preheat the oven to 400°F/200°C. Dampen several large cookie sheets. Thinly roll out the pastry on a lightly floured counter. Using a plain, 3 1/4-inch/8-cm round cutter, cut out 32 circles, rerolling the trimmings as necessary. Using a teaspoon, put an equal, small amount of the tuna mixture in the center of each pastry circle. Dampen the edges of the pastry with a little water and fold one half over the other to form a crescent and enclose the filling. Pinch the edges together with your fingers to seal, then press with the tines of a fork to seal more securely. Transfer to the prepared cookie sheets.

With the tip of a sharp knife, make a small slit in the top of each pastry and brush with beaten egg to glaze. Bake in the preheated oven for 15 minutes, or until risen and golden brown. Serve warm.

SERVES 16
as part of a tapas meal

6 oz/175 g canned tuna in
   olive oil
1 small onion, finely chopped
1 garlic clove, finely chopped
1 3/4 oz/50 g pimiento-stuffed
   Spanish olives, finely chopped
heaping 1/8 cup pine nuts
1 lb 2 oz/500 g prepared puff
   pastry, thawed if frozen
all-purpose flour, for dusting
beaten egg, for glazing
salt and pepper

tuna with pimiento-stuffed olives

SERVES 6
as part of a tapas meal

2 fresh tuna steaks, weighing
　about 9 oz/250 g in total and
　about 1 inch/2.5 cm thick
5 tbsp Spanish olive oil
3 tbsp red wine vinegar
4 sprigs of fresh thyme, plus
　extra to garnish
1 bay leaf
2 tbsp all-purpose flour
1 onion, finely chopped
2 garlic cloves, finely chopped
1/2 cup pimiento-stuffed green
　olives, sliced
salt and pepper
crusty bread, to serve

Don't get caught out with this recipe—the tuna steaks need to be
marinated, so remember to start preparing the dish the day before you
are going to serve it. Remove the skin from the tuna steaks, then cut the
steaks in half along the grain of the fish. Cut each half into 1/2-inch/1-cm
thick slices against the grain.

　Put 3 tablespoons of the oil and the vinegar in a large, shallow,
nonmetallic dish. Strip the leaves from the sprigs of thyme and add
these to the dish with the bay leaf and salt and pepper to taste. Add
the prepared strips of tuna, cover the dish, and let marinate in the
refrigerator for 8 hours or overnight.

　The next day, put the flour in a plastic bag. Remove the tuna strips from
the marinade, reserving the marinade for later, add them to the bag of
flour and toss well until they are lightly coated.

　Heat the remaining oil in a large, heavy-bottom skillet. Add the onion
and garlic and gently cook for 5–10 minutes, or until softened
and golden brown. Add the tuna strips to the skillet and cook for
2–5 minutes, turning several times, until the fish becomes opaque. Add
the reserved marinade and olives to the skillet and cook for an additional
1–2 minutes, stirring, until the fish is tender and the sauce has thickened.

　Serve the tuna and olives piping hot, garnished with thyme sprigs.
Accompany with chunks or slices of crusty bread for mopping up
the sauce.

seared squid & golden potatoes

SERVES 8
as part of a tapas meal

2 lb 4 oz/1 kg new potatoes
4–6 tbsp Spanish olive oil
1 large onion, thinly sliced
2 garlic cloves, finely chopped
2 lb 4 oz/1 kg cleaned squid
    bodies, thinly sliced
6 tbsp dry white wine
1 small bunch of fresh flat-leaf
    parsley, finely chopped, plus
    extra to garnish
salt and pepper
lemon wedges, to serve

Put the potatoes in a saucepan of lightly salted water and bring to a boil. Reduce the heat and simmer for 20 minutes, or until tender. Drain well.

Heat 4 tablespoons of the oil in a large ovenproof casserole, then add the potatoes and cook over medium heat, stirring occasionally, for 10 minutes, or until beginning to turn brown. Add the onion and cook, stirring occasionally, for 10 minutes, or until golden brown. Add the garlic and cook, stirring, for 30 seconds, until softened. Push all the ingredients to the side of the casserole.

If necessary, add the remaining oil to the casserole. Add the squid slices and cook over high heat, stirring occasionally, for 2 minutes, or until golden brown. Add the wine and cook for an additional 1–2 minutes. Add the parsley and mix the potatoes, onions, and garlic with the squid. Season with salt and pepper to taste.

Serve hot, in the casserole, sprinkled with parsley to garnish and with lemon wedges for squeezing over.

calamari with shrimp & fava beans

Heat the oil in a large skillet with a lid or in an ovenproof casserole. Add the scallions and cook over medium heat, stirring occasionally, for 4–5 minutes, or until softened. Add the garlic and cook, stirring, for 30 seconds, or until softened. Add the squid slices and cook over high heat, stirring occasionally, for 2 minutes, or until golden brown.

Add the wine and bring to a boil. Add the fava beans and reduce the heat, then cover and simmer, for 5–8 minutes if using fresh beans or 4–5 minutes if using frozen beans, until the beans are tender.

Add the shrimp and parsley, re-cover, and simmer for an additional 2–3 minutes, or until the shrimp turn pink and start to curl. Season with salt and pepper to taste. Serve hot, with crusty bread to mop up the juices.

SERVES 4–6
as part of a tapas meal

2 tbsp Spanish olive oil
4 scallions, thinly sliced
2 garlic cloves, finely chopped
1 lb 2 oz/500 g cleaned squid bodies, thickly sliced
$1/3$ cup dry white wine
1 lb 5 oz/600 g fresh young fava beans in their pods, shelled to give about 8 oz/225 g, or 8 oz/225 g frozen baby fava beans
9 oz/250 g raw jumbo shrimp, shelled and deveined
4 tbsp chopped fresh flat-leaf parsley
salt and pepper
crusty bread, to serve

tossed shrimp with bell peppers

SERVES 8
as part of a tapas meal

1 lb 2 oz/500 g raw jumbo
   shrimp, in their shells
2 tbsp Spanish olive oil
2 red bell peppers, cored,
   seeded, and thinly sliced
5 garlic cloves, finely chopped
juice of ½ lemon
6 tbsp dry Spanish sherry
salt and pepper
crusty bread, to serve

Pull off the heads of the shrimp. With your fingers, peel away the shells, leaving the tails intact. Using a sharp knife, make a shallow slit along the length of the back of each shrimp, then use the tip of the knife to lift out the dark vein and discard. Rinse the shrimp under cold running water and pat dry with paper towels.

Heat the oil in a large skillet, then add the bell pepper slices and cook for 10–15 minutes, or until softened. Add the garlic and cook, stirring, for 30 seconds, until softened. Add the shrimp to the skillet and cook, tossing continuously, for 1–2 minutes, or until the shrimp turn pink. Add the lemon juice and sherry and cook for an additional 2 minutes, or until the shrimp begin to curl. Season with salt and pepper to taste.

Serve hot, with chunks or slices of crusty bread to mop up the juices.

sizzling chile shrimp

SERVES 6
as part of a tapas meal

1 lb 2 oz/500 g raw jumbo
  shrimp, in their shells
1 small fresh red chile
6 tbsp Spanish olive oil
2 garlic cloves, finely chopped
pinch of paprika
salt
crusty bread, to serve

Pull the heads off the shrimp and peel, leaving the tails intact. Cut along the length of the back of each shrimp and remove and discard the dark vein. Rinse the shrimp under cold running water and pat dry on paper towels.

Cut the chile in half lengthwise, then remove the seeds and finely chop the flesh.

Heat the oil in a large, heavy-bottom skillet or flameproof casserole until quite hot, then add the garlic and cook for 30 seconds. Add the shrimp, chile, paprika, and a pinch of salt and cook for 2–3 minutes, stirring continuously, until the shrimp turn pink and begin to curl.

Serve the shrimp in the cooking dish, still sizzling. Accompany with wooden toothpicks, to spear the shrimp, and chunks or slices of crusty bread to mop up the aromatic cooking oil.

saffron shrimp with lemon mayonnaise

First make the mayonnaise. Place the garlic cloves on a cutting board and sprinkle with a little salt, then flatten them with the side of a heavy knife. Finely chop and flatten again.

Transfer the garlic to a food processor or blender and add the egg yolks, lemon juice, and lemon rind. Process briefly until just blended. With the motor still running, gradually add the corn oil through the feeder tube until it is fully incorporated. Scrape the mayonnaise into a serving bowl and season with salt and pepper to taste, then cover and let chill until ready to serve.

Pull the heads off the shrimp and peel, leaving the tails intact. Cut along the length of the back of each shrimp and remove and discard the dark vein. Rinse under cold running water and pat dry with paper towels.

Sift the flour into a bowl. Mix the beer, oil, and saffron together in a pitcher, then gradually whisk into the flour. Cover and let stand at room temperature for 30 minutes to rest.

Whisk the egg whites in a spotlessly clean, greasefree bowl until stiff. Gently fold the egg whites into the flour mixture.

Heat the vegetable oil in a deep-fat fryer or large saucepan to 350–375°F/180–190°C, or until a cube of bread browns in 30 seconds. Holding the shrimp by their tails, dip them into the batter and shake off any excess. Add the shrimp to the oil and deep-fry for 2–3 minutes, or until crisp. Remove with a slotted spoon and drain well on paper towels. Serve immediately with the lemon mayonnaise.

SERVES 6–8
as part of a tapas meal

2 lb 12 oz/1.25 kg raw
   jumbo shrimp
heaping 1/2 cup all-purpose
   flour
1/2 cup light beer
2 tbsp Spanish olive oil
pinch of saffron powder
2 egg whites
vegetable oil, for deep-frying

lemon mayonnaise
4 garlic cloves
2 egg yolks
1 tbsp lemon juice
1 tbsp finely grated lemon rind
11/4 cups corn oil
sea salt and pepper

lime-drizzled shrimp

SERVES 6
as part of a tapas meal

4 limes
12 raw jumbo shrimp, in their
   shells
3 tbsp Spanish olive oil
2 garlic cloves, finely chopped
splash of fino sherry
4 tbsp chopped fresh
   flat-leaf parsley
salt and pepper

Grate the rind and squeeze the juice from 2 of the limes. Cut the remaining 2 limes into wedges and set aside for later.

To prepare the shrimp, remove the head and legs, leaving the shells and tails intact. Using a sharp knife, make a shallow slit along the back of each shrimp, then pull out the dark vein and discard. Rinse the shrimp under cold running water and dry well on paper towels.

Heat the oil in a large, heavy-bottom skillet, then add the garlic and cook for 30 seconds. Add the shrimp and cook for 5 minutes, stirring occasionally, or until they turn pink and start to curl. Mix in the lime rind, lime juice, and a splash of sherry to moisten, then stir well together.

Transfer the cooked shrimp to a serving dish, season with salt and pepper to taste, and sprinkle with the parsley. Serve piping hot, accompanied by the reserved lime wedges for squeezing over the shrimp.

crab tartlets

SERVES 12
as part of a tapas meal

1 tbsp Spanish olive oil
1 small onion, finely chopped
1 garlic clove, finely chopped
splash of dry white wine
2 eggs
2/3 cup milk or light cream
6 oz/175 g canned crabmeat,
    drained
2 oz/55 g Manchego or
    Parmesan cheese, grated
2 tbsp chopped fresh flat-leaf
    parsley
pinch of freshly grated nutmeg
salt and pepper
fresh dill sprigs, to garnish

pie dough
2 1/3 cups all-purpose flour,
    plus extra for dusting
pinch of salt
3/4 cup butter
2 tbsp cold water

or

1 lb 2 oz/500 g prepared
    unsweetened pie pastry

Preheat the oven to 375°F/190°C. To prepare the crabmeat filling, heat the oil in a saucepan. Add the onion and cook for 5 minutes, or until softened but not browned. Add the garlic and cook for an additional 30 seconds. Add a splash of white wine and cook for 1–2 minutes, or until most of the wine has evaporated.

Lightly whisk the eggs in a large bowl, then whisk in the milk or cream. Add the crabmeat, grated cheese, parsley, and the onion mixture. Season the mixture with nutmeg and salt and pepper to taste and mix together.

To prepare the pie dough, mix the flour and salt together in a large bowl. Add the butter, cut into small pieces, and rub it in until the mixture resembles fine breadcrumbs. Gradually stir in enough of the water to form a firm dough.

Thinly roll out the dough on a lightly floured counter. Using a plain, round 2 3/4-inch/7-cm cutter, cut into 18 circles. Gently pile the trimmings together and roll out again, then cut out an additional 6 circles. Use to line twenty-four 1 1/2-inch/4-cm tartlet pans. Carefully spoon the crabmeat mixture into the tart shells, taking care not to overfill them.

Bake the tartlets in the preheated oven for 25–30 minutes, or until golden brown and set. Serve the crab tartlets hot or cold, garnished with fresh dill sprigs.

sweet peppers stuffed with crab salad

First make the crab salad. Pick over the crabmeat and remove any bits of shell. Put half the crabmeat in a food processor with the prepared red bell pepper, 1 1/2 tablespoons of the lemon juice, and salt and pepper to taste. Process until well blended, then transfer to a bowl. Stir in the cream cheese and remaining crabmeat. Taste and add extra lemon juice, if needed.

Pat the pimientos del piquillo dry and scoop out any seeds that remain in the tips. Use a small spoon to divide the crab salad equally among the pimientos, stuffing them generously. Arrange on a large serving dish or individual plates, then cover and let chill until ready to serve. Just before serving, sprinkle the stuffed pimientos with the chopped parsley.

SERVES 8
as part of a tapas meal

16 pimientos del piquillo,
    drained, or freshly roasted
    sweet peppers, tops cut off
chopped fresh parsley,
    to garnish

crab salad
8 1/2 oz/240 g canned crabmeat,
    drained and squeezed dry
1 red bell pepper, roasted,
    peeled, and chopped
about 2 tbsp fresh lemon juice
scant 1 cup cream cheese
salt and pepper

scallops with serrano ham

SERVES 4
as part of a tapas meal

2 tbsp lemon juice
3 tbsp Spanish olive oil
2 garlic cloves, finely chopped
1 tbsp chopped fresh parsley
12 shelled scallops, preferably
   with corals
8 wafer-thin slices serrano ham
pepper

Mix the lemon juice, olive oil, garlic, and parsley together in a nonmetallic dish. Separate the corals, if using, from the scallops and add both to the dish, turning to coat. Cover with plastic wrap and let marinate at room temperature for 20 minutes.

Preheat the broiler to medium. Drain the scallops, reserving the marinade. Thread a scallop and a coral, if using, on to a metal skewer. Scrunch up a slice of ham and thread on to the skewer, followed by another scallop and a coral. Repeat to fill 4 skewers, each with 3 scallops and 2 slices of ham.

Cook under the hot broiler, basting with the marinade and turning frequently, for 5 minutes, or until the scallops are tender and the ham is crisp.

Transfer to warmed serving plates and sprinkle them with pepper. Spoon over the cooking juices from the broiler pan and serve.

mussels in a vinaigrette dressing

SERVES 6
as part of a tapas meal

6 tbsp Spanish extra virgin
  olive oil
2 tbsp white wine vinegar
1 shallot, finely chopped
1 garlic clove, crushed
2 tbsp capers, chopped
1 fresh red chile, seeded and
  finely chopped (optional)
2 lb 4 oz/1 kg live mussels,
  in their shells
6 tbsp dry white wine
4 tbsp chopped fresh flat-leaf
  parsley
salt and pepper
crusty bread, to serve (optional)

To make the dressing, put the oil and vinegar in a bowl and whisk together. Stir in the shallot, garlic, capers, and chile, if using. Season with salt and pepper to taste.

Clean the mussels by scrubbing or scraping the shells and pulling out any beards that are attached to them. Discard any with broken shells or any that refuse to close when tapped. Put the mussels in a colander and rinse well under cold running water.

Put the mussels in a large saucepan and add the wine. Bring to a boil, then cover and cook over high heat, shaking the pan occasionally, for 3–4 minutes, or until the mussels have opened. Drain the mussels, discarding any that remain closed, and let cool.

When the mussels are cool enough to handle, discard the empty half-shells and arrange the mussels, in their other half-shells, in a large, shallow serving dish. Discard any mussels that remain closed. Whisk the dressing again and spoon over the mussels. Cover and let chill in the refrigerator for at least 1 hour.

To serve, sprinkle the parsley over the mussels and serve with crusty bread, if using, to mop up the dressing.

mussels with garlic butter

Clean the mussels by scrubbing or scraping the shells and pulling out any beards that are attached to them. Discard any with broken shells and any that refuse to close when sharply tapped with the back of a knife. Place the mussels in a colander and rinse under cold running water.

Place the mussels in a large saucepan and add a splash of wine and the bay leaf. Cook, covered, over high heat for 5 minutes, shaking the pan occasionally, or until the mussels are opened. Drain the mussels and discard any that remain closed.

Shell the mussels, reserving one half of each shell. Arrange the mussels, in their half-shells, in a large, shallow, ovenproof serving dish.

Melt the butter and pour into a bowl. Add the breadcrumbs, parsley, chives, and garlic and season with salt and pepper to taste, then mix well together. Let stand until the butter has set slightly. Using your fingers or 2 teaspoons, take a large pinch of the herb and butter mixture and use to fill each mussel shell, pressing it down well. Let the mussels chill until ready to serve.

To serve, preheat the oven to 450°F/230°C. Bake the mussels in the preheated oven for 10 minutes, or until hot. Serve immediately, garnished with parsley and accompanied by lemon wedges for squeezing over.

SERVES 8
as part of a tapas meal

1 lb 12 oz/800 g live mussels,
   in their shells
splash of dry white wine
1 bay leaf
1/2 cup butter
12 oz/350 g fresh white or
   whole wheat breadcrumbs
4 tbsp chopped fresh flat-leaf
   parsley, plus extra sprigs
   to garnish
2 tbsp snipped fresh chives
2 garlic cloves, finely chopped
salt and pepper
lemon wedges, to serve

oysters with sherry vinegar

SERVES 6
as part of a tapas meal

1 shallot, finely chopped
3 tbsp sherry vinegar
3 tbsp red wine vinegar
1 tbsp sugar
24 fresh oysters
pepper
rock salt or crushed ice,
    to serve (optional)

Mix the shallot, vinegars, and sugar together in a nonmetallic bowl and season well with pepper. Cover with plastic wrap and let stand at room temperature for at least 15 minutes so that the flavors mingle.

Meanwhile, shuck the oysters. Wrap a dish towel around your hand to protect it and hold an oyster firmly. Insert an oyster knife or other strong, sharp knife into the hinged edge and twist to pry the shells apart. Still holding both shells firmly in the wrapped hand, slide the blade of the knife along the upper shell to sever the muscle. Lift off the upper shell, being careful not to spill the liquid inside. Slide the blade of the knife along the lower shell underneath the oyster to sever the second muscle. Arrange the oysters on their half shells in a single layer on a bed of rock salt, if using.

Spoon the dressing evenly over the oysters and serve at room temperature.

clams in tomato & garlic sauce

SERVES 6–8
as part of a tapas meal

2 hard-cooked eggs, cooled,
   shelled, and halved lengthwise
3 tbsp Spanish olive oil
1 Spanish onion, chopped
2 garlic cloves, finely chopped
1 lb 9 oz/700 g tomatoes,
   peeled and diced
3/4 cup fresh white
   breadcrumbs
2 lb 4 oz/1 kg fresh clams
13/4 cups dry white wine
2 tbsp chopped fresh parsley
salt and pepper
lemon wedges, to garnish

Scoop out the egg yolks using a teaspoon and rub through a fine strainer into a bowl. Chop the whites and reserve separately.

Heat the oil in a large, heavy-bottom skillet. Add the onion and cook over low heat, stirring occasionally, for 5 minutes, or until softened. Add the garlic and cook for an additional 3 minutes, then add the tomatoes, breadcrumbs, and egg yolks and season with salt and pepper to taste. Cook, stirring occasionally and mashing the mixture with a wooden spoon, for an additional 10–15 minutes, or until thick and pulpy.

Meanwhile, scrub the clams under cold running water. Discard any with broken shells or any that do not close immediately when sharply tapped with the back of a knife.

Place the clams in a large, heavy-bottom saucepan. Add the wine and bring to a boil. Cover and cook over high heat, shaking the pan occasionally, for 3–5 minutes, or until the clams have opened. Discard any that remain closed.

Using a slotted spoon, transfer the clams to warmed serving bowls. Strain the cooking liquid into the tomato sauce, then stir well and spoon over the clams. Sprinkle with the chopped egg whites and parsley and serve immediately, garnished with lemon wedges.

eggs & cheese

Eggs and cheese are two essential ingredients in Spanish cooking, offering

great scope for many inexpensive tapas recipes. Nothing symbolizes the

essence of tapas more than the thick egg and potato omelet known as

Spanish Tortilla. Made with such humble ingredients and once a meager meal

for poor laborers, it is now the nation's favorite tapas. This chapter contains

many satisfying variations, but whichever you try, it will be delicious hot or at

room temperature. Oven-Baked Tortilla, cut into tiny squares and speared on

toothpicks, makes a good party dish. Cheese Puffs with Fiery Tomato Salsa

are perennially popular, while Figs with Bleu Cheese make good use of

wonderfully fresh ingredients.

spanish tortilla

SERVES 8
as part of a tapas meal

¹/₂ cup Spanish olive oil
1 lb 5 oz/600 g potatoes, peeled
   and thinly sliced
1 large onion, thinly sliced
6 large eggs
salt and pepper
fresh flat-leaf parsley,
   to garnish

Heat a nonstick 10-inch/25-cm skillet over high heat. Add the olive oil and heat. Reduce the heat, then add the potatoes and onion and cook for 15–20 minutes, or until the potatoes are tender.

Beat the eggs in a large bowl and season generously with salt and pepper. Drain the potatoes and onion through a strainer over a heatproof bowl to reserve the oil. Very gently stir the vegetables into the eggs, then let stand for 10 minutes.

Use a wooden spoon or spatula to remove any crusty bits stuck to the bottom of the skillet. Reheat the skillet over medium heat with 4 tablespoons of the reserved oil.

Add the egg mixture and smooth the surface, pressing the potatoes and onions into an even layer.

Cook for 5 minutes, shaking the skillet occasionally, until the bottom is set. Use a spatula to loosen the side of the tortilla. Place a large plate over the top and carefully invert the skillet and plate together so the tortilla drops onto the plate.

Add 1 tablespoon of the remaining reserved oil to the skillet and swirl around. Carefully slide the tortilla back into the skillet, cooked-side up. Run the spatula around the tortilla, to tuck in the edge.

Continue cooking for 3 minutes, or until the eggs are set and the base is golden brown. Remove the skillet from the heat and slide the tortilla onto a plate. Let stand for at least 5 minutes before cutting. Garnish with parsley and serve.

oven–baked tortilla

SERVES 16
as part of a tapas meal

4 tbsp Spanish olive oil, plus
    extra for oiling
1 large garlic clove, crushed
4 scallions, white and green
    parts finely chopped
1 green bell pepper, seeded
    and finely diced
1 red bell pepper, seeded and
    finely diced
6 oz/175 g potato, boiled,
    peeled, and diced
5 large eggs
scant 1/2 cup sour cream
6 oz/175 g Spanish Rocal,
    cheddar, or Parmesan
    cheese, grated
3 tbsp snipped fresh chives
salt and pepper
slices of bread and
green salad, to serve

Preheat the oven to 375°F/190°C. Line a 7 × 10-inch/18 × 25-cm baking sheet with foil and brush with a little oil. Reserve.

Place the oil, garlic, scallions, and bell peppers in a skillet and cook over medium heat, stirring, for 10 minutes, or until the onions are softened but not browned. Let cool, then stir in the potato.

Beat the eggs, sour cream, cheese, and chives together in a large bowl. Stir the cooled vegetables into the bowl and season with salt and pepper to taste.

Pour the mixture onto the baking sheet and smooth over the top. Bake in the preheated oven for 30–40 minutes, or until golden brown, puffed, and set in the center. Remove from the oven and let cool and set. Run a spatula around the edge, then invert onto a cutting board, browned-side up, and peel off the foil. If the surface looks a little runny, place it under a medium broiler to dry out.

Let cool completely. Trim the edges if necessary, then cut into 48 squares. Serve on a platter with wooden toothpicks, or secure each square to a slice of bread, and accompany with a green salad.

chorizo & fava bean tortilla

Bring a saucepan of lightly salted water to a boil, add the beans, and cook for 4 minutes. Drain well and let cool. Meanwhile, lightly beat the eggs in a large bowl. Add the chorizo sausage and season with salt and pepper to taste.

When the beans are cool enough to handle, slip off their skins. This is a laborious task, but worth doing if you have the time. This quantity will take about 15 minutes to skin.

Heat the oil in a large skillet, then add the onion and cook over medium heat, stirring occasionally, for 5 minutes, or until softened but not browned. Add the beans and cook, stirring, for 1 minute. Pour the egg mixture into the skillet and cook gently for 2–3 minutes, or until the underside is just set and lightly browned. Use a spatula to loosen the tortilla away from the side and bottom of the skillet to let the uncooked egg run underneath and prevent the tortilla from sticking to the bottom.

Cover the tortilla with a large, upside-down plate and invert the tortilla onto it. Slide the tortilla back into the skillet, cooked-side up, and cook for an additional 2–3 minutes, or until the underside is lightly browned.

Slide the tortilla onto a warmed serving dish. Serve warm, cut into small cubes.

SERVES 8
as part of a tapas meal

8 oz/225 g frozen baby
    fava beans
6 eggs
3 1/2 oz/100 g chorizo sausage,
    outer casing removed,
    chopped
3 tbsp Spanish olive oil
1 onion, chopped
salt and pepper

spinach & mushroom tortilla

SERVES 8
as part of a tapas meal

2 tbsp Spanish olive oil
3 shallots, finely chopped
12 oz/350 g mushrooms, sliced
10 oz/280 g fresh spinach
   leaves, coarse stems
   removed
2 oz/55 g toasted slivered
   almonds
5 eggs
2 tbsp chopped fresh parsley
2 tbsp cold water
3 oz/85 g mature Mahon,
   Manchego, or Parmesan
   cheese, grated
salt and pepper

Heat the oil in a skillet that can safely be placed under the broiler. Add the shallots and cook over low heat, stirring occasionally, for 5 minutes, or until softened. Add the mushrooms and cook, stirring frequently, for an additional 4 minutes. Add the spinach, then increase the heat to medium and cook, stirring frequently, for 3–4 minutes, or until wilted. Reduce the heat, then season with salt and pepper to taste and stir in the almonds.

Beat the eggs with the parsley, water, and salt and pepper to taste in a bowl. Pour the mixture into the skillet and cook for 5–8 minutes, or until the underside is set. Lift the edge of the tortilla occasionally to let the uncooked egg run underneath. Meanwhile, preheat the broiler to high.

Sprinkle the grated cheese over the tortilla and cook under the preheated hot broiler for 3 minutes, or until the top is set and the cheese has melted. Serve, lukewarm or cold, cut into thin wedges.

chorizo & cheese tortilla

SERVES 8

2 small potatoes
4 tbsp olive oil
1 small onion, chopped
1 red bell pepper, seeded and
   chopped
2 tomatoes, seeded and diced
5 oz/140 g chorizo sausage,
   finely chopped
8 large eggs
2 tbsp cold water
2 oz/55 g mature Mahon,
   Manchego, or Parmesan
   cheese, grated
salt and pepper

Bring a small saucepan of lightly salted water to a boil, add the potatoes, and cook for 15–20 minutes, or until just tender. Drain and let stand until cool enough to handle, then dice.

Heat the olive oil in a large skillet that can safely be placed under the broiler. Add the onion, bell pepper, and tomatoes and cook over low heat, stirring occasionally, for 5 minutes. Add the diced potatoes and chorizo and cook for an additional 5 minutes. Meanwhile, preheat the broiler to high.

Beat the eggs with the water and salt and pepper to taste in a large bowl. Pour the mixture into the skillet and cook for 8–10 minutes, or until the underside is set. Lift the edge of the tortilla occasionally to let the uncooked egg run underneath. Sprinkle the grated cheese over the tortilla and place under the hot broiler for 3 minutes, or until the top is set and the cheese has melted. Serve, warm or cold, cut into thin wedges.

eggplant tortilla wedges

Cut the eggplants into ¼-inch/5-mm thick slices. Heat 2 tablespoons of the oil in a large skillet, then add the onion and cook over medium heat, stirring occasionally, for 5 minutes, or until softened but not browned. Add the remaining oil to the skillet and heat until hot. Add the eggplant slices and cook over medium heat, turning occasionally, for 15–20 minutes until tender.

Meanwhile, lightly beat the eggs in a large bowl and season generously with salt and pepper. When the eggplants are cooked, drain in a strainer set over a large bowl to catch the oil. When well drained, gently stir into the beaten eggs. Wipe the skillet clean or wash, if necessary, to prevent the tortilla from sticking. Pour the reserved oil into the skillet and heat. Add the egg and eggplant mixture and cook gently for 3–4 minutes, or until the underside is just set and lightly browned. Use a spatula to loosen the tortilla away from the side and bottom of the skillet to let most of the uncooked egg run underneath and prevent the tortilla from sticking to the bottom.

Cover the tortilla with a large, upside-down plate and invert the tortilla onto it. Slide the tortilla back into the skillet, cooked-side up, and cook for an additional 3–4 minutes, or until the underside is lightly browned.

Slide the tortilla onto a warmed serving dish. Cut the tortilla into wedges and serve warm, sprinkled generously with chopped parsley, if using.

SERVES 8–10
as part of a tapas meal

1 lb 2 oz/500 g eggplants
½ cup Spanish olive oil
1 onion, chopped
6 eggs
salt and pepper
chopped fresh flat-leaf parsley,
    to garnish (optional)

deviled eggs

SERVES 8
as part of a tapas meal

8 large eggs
2 whole canned or bottled
  pimientos del piquillo
16 pitted green Spanish olives
5 tbsp mayonnaise
8 drops of Tabasco sauce
large pinch of cayenne pepper
salt and pepper
paprika, for dusting
lettuce leaves, to garnish

To cook the eggs, place them in a saucepan, then cover with cold water and slowly bring to a boil. Immediately reduce the heat to very low, then cover and simmer gently for 10 minutes. As soon as the eggs are cooked, drain and place under cold running water until they are cold. Doing this quickly will prevent a black ring from forming around the egg yolk. Gently tap the eggs to crack the shells and let stand until cold. When cold, crack the shells and remove them.

Using a stainless steel knife, halve the eggs lengthwise, then carefully remove the yolks. Place the yolks in a nylon strainer set over a bowl and rub through, then mash them with a wooden spoon or fork. If necessary, rinse the egg whites under cold running water and dry carefully.

Place the pimientos on paper towels to dry well, then chop them finely, reserving a few strips. Finely chop half of the olives. Halve the remaining olives and reserve. If you are going to pipe the filling into the eggs, you will need to chop both these ingredients very finely so that they will go through a ¹/₂-inch/1-cm nozzle. Add the chopped pimientos and chopped olives to the mashed egg yolks. Add the mayonnaise, mix together well, then add the Tabasco sauce, cayenne pepper, and salt and pepper to taste.

For a grand finale, place the egg yolk mixture into a pastry bag fitted with a ¹/₂-inch/1-cm plain tip and pipe the mixture into the hollow egg whites. Alternatively, for a simpler finish, use a teaspoon to spoon the prepared filling into each egg half.

Arrange the eggs on a serving plate. Add 1–2 small strips of the reserved pimientos and an olive half to the top of each stuffed egg. Dust with a little paprika and garnish with lettuce leaves, then serve.

stuffed eggs with anchovies & cheese

**SERVES 8
as part of a tapas meal**

8 eggs
1³/₄ oz/50 g canned anchovy
  fillets in olive oil, drained
2 oz/55 g Manchego cheese,
  grated
4 tbsp Spanish extra virgin
  olive oil
1 tbsp freshly squeezed lemon
  juice
1 garlic clove, crushed
4 pitted black Spanish olives,
  halved
4 pitted green Spanish olives,
  halved
hot or sweet smoked Spanish
  paprika, for dusting
salt and pepper

Put the eggs in a saucepan, then cover with cold water and slowly bring to a boil. Reduce the heat and simmer gently for 10 minutes. Immediately drain the eggs and rinse under cold running water to cool. Gently tap the eggs to crack the shells and let stand until cold.

When the eggs are cold, crack the shells all over and remove them. Using a stainless steel knife, halve the eggs, then carefully remove the egg yolks and put in a food processor.

Add the anchovy fillets, cheese, oil, lemon juice, and garlic to the egg yolks and process to a puree. Season with salt and pepper to taste.

Using a teaspoon, spoon the mixture into the egg white halves. Alternatively, using a pastry bag fitted with a ¹/₂-inch/1-cm plain tip, pipe the mixture into the egg white halves. Arrange the eggs in a serving dish, then cover and chill in the refrigerator until ready to serve.

To serve, put an olive half on the top of each stuffed egg and dust with paprika.

eggs & cheese

Cut the eggs in half lengthwise and, using a teaspoon, carefully scoop out the yolks into a fine strainer, reserving the egg white halves. Rub the yolks through the strainer into a bowl and add the cheese, mayonnaise, chives, chile, and salt and pepper to taste.

Spoon the filling into the egg white halves.

Arrange a bed of lettuce on individual serving plates and top with the eggs. Cover and let chill until ready to serve.

SERVES 6
as part of a tapas meal

6 hard-cooked eggs, cooled and
    shelled
3 tbsp grated Manchego or
    cheddar cheese
1–2 tbsp mayonnaise
2 tbsp snipped fresh chives
1 fresh red chile, seeded and
    finely chopped
salt and pepper
lettuce leaves, to serve

asparagus & fried eggs

SERVES 6
as part of a tapas meal

1 lb 2 oz/500 g asparagus
   spears
2 tbsp Spanish olive oil
6 eggs

Trim and discard the coarse, woody ends of the asparagus spears. Make sure all the stems are about the same length, then tie them together loosely with clean kitchen string. If you have an asparagus steamer, you don't need to tie the stems together—just place them in the basket.

Bring a tall saucepan of lightly salted water to a boil. Add the asparagus, making sure that the tips are protruding above the water, then reduce the heat and let simmer for 10–15 minutes, or until tender. Test by piercing a stem just above the water level with the point of a sharp knife.

Meanwhile, heat a little of the olive oil in a large, heavy-bottom skillet. Add 2 eggs, if there is enough room, and cook over medium–low heat, or until the whites are just set and the yolks are still runny. Transfer to warmed serving plates and cook the remaining eggs in the same way.

Drain the asparagus and divide the spears among the plates. Serve immediately.

asparagus scrambled eggs

SERVES 6
as part of a tapas meal

1 lb/450 g asparagus, trimmed
   and coarsely chopped
2 tbsp Spanish olive oil
1 onion, finely chopped
1 garlic clove, finely chopped
6 eggs
1 tbsp water
6 small slices country bread
salt and pepper

Steam the asparagus pieces for 8 minutes or cook in a large saucepan of boiling salted water for 4 minutes, or until just tender, depending on their thickness. Drain well, if necessary.

Meanwhile, heat the oil in a large skillet, then add the onion and cook over medium heat, stirring occasionally, for 5 minutes, or until softened but not browned. Add the garlic and cook, stirring, for 30 seconds until softened.

Stir the asparagus into the skillet and cook, stirring occasionally, for 3–4 minutes. Meanwhile, break the eggs into a bowl, then add the water and beat together. Season with salt and pepper to taste.

Preheat the broiler to high. Add the beaten eggs to the asparagus mixture and cook, stirring continuously, for 2 minutes, or until the eggs have just set. Remove from the heat.

Toast the bread slices under the broiler until golden brown on both sides. Pile the scrambled eggs on top of the toast and serve immediately.

basque scrambled eggs

Heat 2 tablespoons of the oil in a large, heavy-bottom skillet over medium–high heat. Add the onion and bell peppers and cook for about 5 minutes, or until the vegetables are softened, but not browned. Add the tomatoes and heat through. Transfer to a plate and keep warm in a preheated low oven.

Add another tablespoon of oil to the skillet. Add the chorizo and cook for 30 seconds, just to warm through and flavor the oil. Add the sausage to the reserved vegetables.

There should be about 2 tablespoons of oil in the skillet, so add a little extra, if necessary, to make up the amount. Add the butter and let melt. Season the eggs with salt and pepper, then add them to the skillet. Scramble the eggs until they are cooked to the desired degree of firmness. Add extra seasoning to taste. Return the vegetables to the skillet and stir through. Serve immediately with hot toast.

SERVES 4–6
as part of a tapas meal

2–4 tbsp Spanish olive oil
1 large onion, finely chopped
1 large red bell pepper, cored, seeded, and chopped
1 large green bell pepper, cored, seeded, and chopped
2 large tomatoes, peeled, seeded, and chopped
2 oz/55 g chorizo sausage, thinly sliced, casings removed, if preferred
3 tbsp butter
10 large eggs, lightly beaten
salt and pepper
4–6 thick slices country-style bread, toasted, to serve

flamenco eggs

SERVES 4
as part of a tapas meal

4 tbsp Spanish olive oil
1 onion, thinly sliced
2 garlic cloves, finely chopped
2 small red bell peppers,
    seeded and chopped
4 tomatoes, peeled, seeded,
    and chopped
1 tbsp chopped fresh parsley
7 oz/200 g canned corn kernels,
    drained
4 eggs
salt and cayenne pepper

Preheat the oven to 350°F/180°C. Heat the oil in a large, heavy-bottom skillet. Add the onion and garlic and cook over low heat, stirring occasionally, for 5 minutes, or until softened. Add the bell peppers and cook, stirring occasionally, for an additional 10 minutes. Stir in the tomatoes and parsley, season with salt and cayenne pepper to taste, and cook for an additional 5 minutes. Stir in the corn kernels and remove the skillet from the heat.

Divide the mixture among 4 individual ovenproof dishes. Make a hollow in the surface of each using the back of a spoon. Break an egg into each depression.

Bake in the preheated oven for 15–25 minutes, or until the eggs have set. Serve hot.

baked tomato nests

SERVES 4
as part of a tapas meal

4 large ripe tomatoes
4 large eggs
4 tbsp heavy cream
4 tbsp grated mature Mahon,
   Manchego, or Parmesan
   cheese
salt and pepper

Preheat the oven to 350°F/180°C. Cut a slice off the tops of the tomatoes and, using a teaspoon, carefully scoop out the pulp and seeds without piercing the shells. Turn the tomato shells upside down on paper towels and let drain for 15 minutes. Season the insides of the shells with salt and pepper.

  Place the tomatoes in an ovenproof dish just large enough to hold them in a single layer. Carefully break 1 egg into each tomato shell, then top with 1 tablespoon of cream and 1 tablespoon of grated cheese.

  Bake in the preheated oven for 15–20 minutes, or until the eggs are just set. Serve hot.

cheese puffs with fiery tomato salsa

To make the salsa, heat the oil in a saucepan. Add the onion and cook for 5 minutes, or until softened but not browned. Add the garlic and cook for an additional 30 seconds. Add the wine and let bubble, then add all the remaining salsa ingredients to the pan and simmer, uncovered, for 10–15 minutes, or until a thick sauce has formed. Spoon into a serving bowl and reserve until ready to serve.

Meanwhile, prepare the cheese puffs. Sift the flour onto a plate or sheet of wax paper. Place the oil and water in a saucepan and slowly bring to a boil. As soon as the water boils, remove from the heat and quickly add the flour all at once. Using a wooden spoon, beat the mixture until it is smooth and leaves the side of the pan.

Let the mixture cool for 1–2 minutes. Gradually add the eggs, beating hard after each addition and keeping the mixture stiff. Add the cheese and paprika, then season with salt and pepper to taste and mix well. Store in the refrigerator until you are ready to cook the cheese puffs.

Just before serving the cheese puffs, heat the sunflower oil in a deep-fat fryer to 350–375°F/180–190°C, or until a cube of bread browns in 30 seconds. Drop teaspoonfuls of the prepared mixture, in batches, into the hot oil and deep-fry for 2–3 minutes, turning once, or until golden brown and crispy. They should rise to the surface of the oil and puff up. Drain well on paper towels.

Serve the puffs piping hot, accompanied by the fiery salsa for dipping and wooden toothpicks to spear the puffs.

SERVES 8
as part of a tapas meal

1/2 cup all-purpose flour
1/4 cup Spanish olive oil
2/3 cup water
2 eggs, beaten
2 oz/55 g Manchego, Parmesan, cheddar, Gouda, or Gruyère cheese, finely grated
1/2 tsp paprika
corn oil, for deep-frying
salt and pepper

tomato salsa
2 tbsp Spanish olive oil
1 small onion, finely chopped
1 garlic clove, crushed
splash of dry white wine
14 oz/400 g canned chopped tomatoes
1 tbsp tomato paste
1/4–1/2 tsp chile flakes
dash of Tabasco sauce
pinch of sugar
salt and pepper

fried manchego cheese

SERVES 6–8
as part of a tapas meal

7 oz/200 g Manchego cheese
3 tbsp all-purpose flour
1 egg
1 tsp water
1¹/₂ cups fresh white or whole
 wheat breadcrumbs
corn oil, for deep-frying
salt and pepper

Slice the cheese into triangular shapes about 2 cm/³/₄ inch thick or alternatively into cubes measuring about the same size. Place the flour in a plastic bag and season with salt and pepper to taste. Break the egg into a shallow dish and beat together with the water. Spread out the breadcrumbs on a large plate.

Toss the cheese pieces in the flour so that they are evenly coated, then dip the cheese in the egg mixture. Finally, dip the cheese in the breadcrumbs so that the pieces are coated on all sides. Transfer to a large plate and store in the refrigerator until you are ready to serve them.

Just before serving, heat about 1 inch/2.5 cm of the corn oil in a large, heavy-bottom skillet or deep-fat fryer to 350–375°F/180–190°C, or until a cube of bread browns in 30 seconds. Add the cheese pieces, in batches of about 4 or 5 pieces so that the temperature of the oil does not drop, and deep-fry for 1–2 minutes, turning once, until the cheese is just beginning to melt and they are golden brown on all sides. Make sure that the oil is hot enough, otherwise the coating on the cheese will take too long to become crisp and the cheese inside may ooze out.

Using a slotted spoon, remove the fried cheese from the skillet or deep-fat fryer and drain well on paper towels. Serve the fried cheese pieces hot, accompanied by wooden toothpicks on which to spear them.

bell peppers with fiery cheese

SERVES 6
as part of a tapas meal

1 red bell pepper, halved and
    seeded
1 orange bell pepper, halved
    and seeded
1 yellow bell pepper, halved
    and seeded
4 oz/115 g Afuega'l Pitu cheese
    or other hot spiced cheese,
    diced
1 tbsp clear honey
1 tbsp sherry vinegar
salt and pepper

Preheat the broiler to high. Place the bell peppers, skin-side up, in a single layer on a baking sheet. Cook under the hot broiler for 8–10 minutes, or until the skins have blistered and blackened. Using tongs, transfer to a plastic bag. Tie the top and let cool.

When the bell peppers are cool enough to handle, peel off the skin and discard. Place on a serving plate and sprinkle over the cheese.

Whisk the honey and vinegar together in a bowl and season with salt and pepper to taste. Pour the dressing over the bell peppers, then cover and let chill until ready to serve.

stuffed pimientos

Remove the pimientos from the jar, reserving the oil for later.

To make the Curd Cheese & Herb Filling, put the curd cheese in a bowl and add the lemon juice, garlic, parsley, mint, and oregano. Mix well together. Season with salt and pepper to taste.

To make the Tuna Mayonnaise Filling, put the tuna in a bowl and add the mayonnaise, lemon juice, and parsley. Add 1 tablespoon of the reserved oil from the jar of pimientos and mix well. Season with salt and pepper to taste.

To make the Goat Cheese & Olive Filling, put the olives in a bowl, and add the cheese, garlic, and 1 tablespoon of the reserved oil from the jar of pimientos. Mix well together. Season with salt and pepper to taste.

Using a teaspoon, heap the filling of your choice into each pimiento. Put in the refrigerator and let chill for at least 2 hours until firm.

To serve the pimientos, arrange them on a serving plate and, if necessary, wipe with paper towels to remove any of the filling that has spread over the skins. Garnish with herb sprigs.

SERVES 4
as part of a tapas meal

$6^{1}/_{2}$ oz/185 g canned or bottled whole pimientos del piquillo
salt and pepper
fresh herb sprigs, to garnish

curd cheese & herb filling
1 cup curd cheese
1 tsp lemon juice
1 garlic clove, crushed
4 tbsp chopped fresh flat-leaf parsley
1 tbsp chopped fresh mint
1 tbsp chopped fresh oregano
salt and pepper

tuna mayonnaise filling
7 oz/200 g canned tuna steak in olive oil, drained
5 tbsp mayonnaise
2 tsp lemon juice
2 tbsp chopped fresh flat-leaf parsley
salt and pepper

goat cheese & olive filling
scant $^{1}/_{3}$ cup pitted black olives, finely chopped
7 oz/200 g soft goat cheese
1 garlic clove, crushed
salt and pepper

empanadillas with cheese & olives

**SERVES 6
as part of a tapas meal**

3 oz/85 g firm or soft cheese
$^1/_2$ cup pitted green Spanish
  olives
$^1/_3$ cup sun-dried tomatoes
  in oil, drained
1$^3/_4$ oz/50 g canned anchovy
  fillets, drained
2 oz/55 g sun-dried tomato
  paste
1 lb 2 oz/500 g prepared puff
  pastry, thawed if frozen
all-purpose flour, for dusting
beaten egg, for glazing
pepper

Preheat the oven to 400°F/200°C. Cut the cheese into small dice measuring about $^1/_4$ inch/5 mm. Chop the olives, sun-dried tomatoes, and anchovies into pieces about the same size as the cheese. Place all the chopped ingredients in a bowl, then season with pepper to taste and gently mix together. Stir in the sun-dried tomato paste.

Thinly roll out the puff pastry on a lightly floured counter. Using a plain, round 3$^1/_4$-inch/8-cm cutter, cut into 16 circles. Gently pile the trimmings together and roll out again, then cut out an additional 8 circles. Using a teaspoon, place a little of the prepared filling equally in the center of each of the pastry circles.

Dampen the edges of the pastry with a little water, then bring up the sides to completely cover the filling and pinch the edges together with your fingers to seal them. With the point of a sharp knife, make a small slit in the top of each pastry. You can store the pastries in the refrigerator at this stage until you are ready to bake them.

Place the pastries onto dampened baking sheets and brush each with a little beaten egg to glaze. Bake in the preheated oven for 10–15 minutes, or until golden brown, crisp, and well risen. Serve the empanadillas piping hot, warm, or cold.

sun-dried tomato
& goat cheese tarts

SERVES 6
as part of a tapas meal

2¹/₂ oz/70 g sun-dried tomatoes
    in oil, drained, and 2 tbsp oil
    reserved
1 zucchini, thinly sliced
1 garlic clove, crushed
9 oz/250 g puff pastry,
    thawed if frozen
5¹/₂ oz/150 g soft goat cheese
salt and pepper

Preheat the oven to 425°F/220°C. Dampen a large cookie sheet. Finely chop the sun-dried tomatoes and reserve. Heat 1 tablespoon of the reserved oil from the tomatoes in a large skillet, then add the zucchini slices and cook over medium heat, stirring occasionally, for 8–10 minutes, or until golden brown on both sides. Add the garlic and cook, stirring, for 30 seconds. Remove from the heat and let cool while you prepare the tart shells.

Thinly roll out the pastry on a lightly floured counter. Using a plain, 3¹/₂-inch/9-cm cutter, cut out 1–2 circles, rerolling the trimmings as necessary. Transfer the circles to the prepared cookie sheet and prick 3–4 times with the tines of a fork. Divide the zucchini mixture equally among the pastry circles, add the tomatoes, leaving a ¹/₂-inch/1-cm border around the edge, and top each tart with a spoonful of goat cheese. Drizzle over 1 tablespoon of the remaining oil from the tomatoes and season with salt and pepper to taste.

Bake the tarts in the preheated oven for 10–15 minutes, or until golden brown and well risen. Serve warm.

figs with bleu cheese

First make the caramelized almonds. Lightly grease a baking sheet with a little butter. Place the sugar in a saucepan over medium heat and stir until the sugar melts and turns golden brown and bubbles. Do not stir once the mixture begins to bubble. Remove the pan from the heat, then add the almonds one at a time and quickly turn with a fork until coated. If the caramel hardens, return the pan to the heat. Transfer each almond to the prepared baking sheet once it is coated. Let stand until cool and firm.

To serve, slice the figs in half and arrange 4 halves on individual serving plates. Coarsely chop the almonds by hand. Place a mound of bleu cheese on each plate and sprinkle with chopped almonds. Drizzle the figs very lightly with the olive oil.

SERVES 6
as part of a tapas meal

12 ripe figs
12 oz/350 g Spanish bleu
   cheese, such as Picós,
   crumbled
Spanish extra virgin olive oil,
   for drizzling

caramelized almonds
1/2 cup superfine sugar
4 oz/115 g blanched almonds
butter, for greasing

bleu cheese & bean salad

SERVES 4
as part of a tapas meal

scant 1 cup small dried
   cannellini beans, soaked for
   4 hours or overnight
1 bay leaf
4 tbsp Spanish olive oil
2 tbsp sherry vinegar
2 tsp clear honey
1 tsp Dijon mustard
2 tbsp toasted slivered almonds
7 oz/200 g Cabrales or other
   bleu cheese, crumbled
salt and pepper

Drain the beans and place in a large, heavy-bottom pan. Pour in enough water to cover, then add the bay leaf and bring to a boil. Boil for 1–1 1/2 hours, or until tender. Drain, then turn into a bowl and let cool slightly. Remove and discard the bay leaf.

Meanwhile, make the dressing. Whisk the oil, vinegar, honey, and mustard together in a bowl and season with salt and pepper to taste. Pour the dressing over the beans and toss lightly. Add the almonds and toss lightly again. Let cool to room temperature.

Spoon the beans into individual serving bowls and scatter over the cheese before serving.

russian salad

SERVES 8
as part of a tapas meal

2 eggs
1 lb/450 g baby new potatoes,
    quartered
4 oz/115 g fine green beans,
    cut into 1-inch/2.5-cm
    lengths
1 cup frozen peas
4 oz/115 g carrots
7 oz/200 g canned tuna steak in
    olive oil, drained
2 tbsp lemon juice
8 tbsp mayonnaise
1 garlic clove, crushed
4 small gherkins, sliced
8 pitted black olives, halved
1 tbsp capers
1 tbsp chopped fresh
    flat-leaf parsley
1 tbsp chopped fresh dill, plus
    extra sprigs to garnish
salt and pepper

Put the eggs in a saucepan, cover with cold water, and slowly bring to a boil. Immediately reduce the heat to very low, cover and let simmer gently for 10 minutes. As soon as the eggs are cooked, drain them and place them under cold running water to cool. Doing this quickly will prevent a black ring from forming round the egg yolk. Gently tap the eggs to crack the shells and let stand until cold.

Meanwhile, put the potatoes in a large saucepan of cold, lightly salted water and bring to a boil. Reduce the heat and let simmer for 7 minutes, or until just tender. Add the beans and peas to the pan for the last 2 minutes of cooking. Drain well, splash under cold running water, then let the vegetables cool completely.

Cut the carrots into julienne strips about 1 inch/2.5 cm in length. Flake the tuna into large chunks. When the potatoes, beans, and peas are cold, put them in a large bowl. Add the carrot strips and the flaked tuna and very gently toss the ingredients together. Transfer the vegetables and tuna to a salad bowl or large serving dish.

In a pitcher, stir the lemon juice into the mayonnaise to thin it slightly, then stir in the garlic and season with salt and pepper to taste. Drizzle the mayonnaise dressing over the vegetables and tuna.

Sprinkle the gherkins, olives, and capers into the salad and finally sprinkle over the parsley and dill. You can store the salad in the refrigerator but return to room temperature before serving. Just before serving, crack the shells of the eggs all over and remove them. Slice the eggs into wedges, add them to the salad, and garnish with dill sprigs.

bread

Bread and tapas are a culinary marriage made in heaven. Spaniards don't consider a meal complete without bread, and tapas are no exception. In Barcelona, for example, it's second nature to have a slice of Tomato Bread when stopping at a bar. Visit any tapas bar throughout the country and there will be a selection of salads on bread—creamy mayonnaise-based salads, such as tuna salad, potato salad, or tender flakes of salt cod. In this chapter you will find plenty of ideas for quick and easy toast toppings as well as a selection of delicious dips and pâtés. There are also recipes for Spanish-style flatbreads and pizzas, not to mention Chorizo Bread Parcels—tiny balls of dough with a meaty filling.

catalan toasts

SERVES 8
as part of a tapas meal

2 garlic cloves
2 large tomatoes
8 slices day-old French bread
   or small rounds of country
   bread or sourdough bread,
   about 3/4 inch/2 cm thick
choice of toppings such as
   slices of serrano ham, slices
   of Manchego cheese, or
   pieces of roasted red bell
   pepper (optional)
3 tbsp Spanish extra virgin
   olive oil
pepper

Preheat the broiler to high. Halve the garlic cloves. Coarsely grate the tomatoes into a bowl, discarding the skins left in your hand, and season with pepper to taste.

Toast the bread slices under the broiler until lightly golden brown on both sides. While the bread slices are still warm, rub with the cut side of the garlic halves to flavor, then top with the grated tomatoes. If using, add a slice of ham or cheese or a piece of roasted bell pepper. Drizzle each with a little oil and serve immediately.

chorizo bread pockets

SERVES 4
as part of a tapas meal

scant 1¹/₂ cups white bread
  flour, plus extra for dusting
1¹/₂ tsp active dry yeast
¹/₂ tsp salt
¹/₄ tsp superfine sugar
¹/₂ cup warm water
sunflower oil, for oiling
4 oz/115 g chorizo sausage,
  outer casing removed
Aïoli (see page 58), to serve

To make the bread dough, put the flour, yeast, salt, and sugar in a large bowl and make a well in the center. Pour the water into the well and gradually mix in the flour from the side. Using your hands, mix together to form a soft dough that leaves the side of the bowl clean.

Turn the dough on to a lightly floured counter and knead for 10 minutes, or until smooth and elastic and no longer sticky. Shape the dough into a ball and put in a clean bowl. Cover with a clean, damp dish towel and let stand in a warm place for 1 hour, or until the dough has risen and doubled in size.

Preheat the oven to 400°F/200°C. Oil a cookie sheet. Cut the chorizo sausage into 16 equal-size chunks. Turn out the risen dough on to a lightly floured counter and knead lightly for 2–3 minutes to knock out the air.

Divide the dough into 16 equal-size pieces. Shape each piece into a ball and roll out on a lightly floured counter to a 4¹/₂-inch/12-cm circle. Put a piece of chorizo on each circle and gather the dough at the top, enclosing the chorizo, then pinch the edges together well to seal. Put each dough pocket, pinched-side down, on the prepared cookie sheet.

Bake in the preheated oven for 20 minutes, or until pale golden brown. Turn the pockets over so that the pinched ends are facing up and arrange in a serving basket. Serve hot, with a bowl of aïoli for dipping, as soon after baking as possible, because the pockets become dry on standing.

spicy fried bread
& chorizo

Cut the chorizo into $^1/_2$-inch/1-cm thick slices and cut the bread, with its crusts still on, into $^1/_2$-inch/1-cm cubes. Add enough oil to a large, heavy-bottom skillet to generously cover the base. Heat the oil, then add the garlic and cook for 30–60 seconds, or until lightly browned.

Add the bread cubes to the skillet and cook, stirring continuously, until golden brown and crisp. Add the chorizo slices and cook for 1–2 minutes, or until hot. Using a slotted spoon, remove the bread cubes and chorizo from the skillet and drain well on paper towels.

Turn the bread and chorizo into a warmed serving bowl, then add the chopped parsley and toss together. Garnish the dish with a sprinkling of paprika and serve warm. Accompany with wooden toothpicks so that a piece of sausage and a cube of bread can be speared together for eating.

SERVES 6–8
as part of a tapas meal

7 oz/200 g chorizo sausage,
  outer casing removed
4 thick slices 2-day-old country
  bread
Spanish olive oil, for pan-frying
3 garlic cloves, finely chopped
2 tbsp chopped fresh flat-leaf
  parsley
paprika, to garnish

chorizo & quail egg toasts

SERVES 6
as part of a tapas meal

12 slices French bread, sliced
   on the diagonal, about
   1/4 inch/5 mm thick
about 1 1/2 oz/40 g cured,
   ready-to-eat chorizo, cut into
   thin slices
olive oil
12 quail eggs
mild paprika
salt and pepper

Preheat the broiler to high. Arrange the slices of bread on a baking sheet and broil until golden brown on both sides.

Cut or fold the chorizo slices to fit on the toasts; set aside. Heat a thin layer of oil in a large skillet over medium heat until a cube of day-old bread sizzles—this takes about 40 seconds. Break the eggs into the skillet and cook, spooning the fat over the yolks, until the whites are set and the yolks are cooked to your liking.

Remove the cooked eggs from the skillet and drain on paper towels. Immediately transfer to the chorizo-topped toasts and dust with paprika. Sprinkle with salt and pepper to taste, and serve at once.

salt cod on garlic toasts

SERVES 6
as part of a tapas meal

7 oz/200 g dried salt cod
5 garlic cloves
1 cup olive oil
1 cup heavy cream
6 thick slices country bread
pepper

Soak the salt cod in cold water for 48 hours, changing the water 3 times a day. Drain well, then cut into chunks and place in a large, shallow skillet. Pour in enough cold water to cover and bring to a simmer. Poach for 8–10 minutes, or until tender. Drain well and let stand until cool enough to handle.

Finely chop 4 of the garlic cloves. Halve the remaining clove and reserve until needed.

Remove the skin from the fish and discard. Coarsely chop the flesh and place in a food processor or blender.

Pour the oil into a saucepan and add the chopped garlic. Bring to a simmer over low heat. Pour the cream into a separate saucepan and bring to a simmer over low heat. Remove both pans from the heat.

Process the fish briefly. With the motor still running, add a little of the garlic oil and process. With the motor still running, add a little cream and process. Continue in this way until all the garlic oil and cream have been incorporated. Scrape the mixture into a serving bowl and season with pepper to taste.

Toast the bread on both sides, then rub each slice with the cut sides of the reserved garlic. Pile the fish mixture onto the toasts and serve.

shrimp & bean toasties

Halve 1 of the garlic cloves and reserve. Finely chop the remaining cloves. Heat 2 tablespoons of the olive oil in a large, heavy-bottom skillet. Add the chopped garlic and onion and cook over low heat, stirring occasionally, for 5 minutes, or until softened.

Stir in the beans and tomatoes and season with salt and pepper to taste. Cook gently for an additional 5 minutes.

Meanwhile, toast the bread on both sides, then rub each slice with the cut sides of the reserved garlic and drizzle with the remaining oil.

Stir the shrimp into the bean mixture and heat through gently for 2–3 minutes. Pile the bean and shrimp mixture onto the toasts and serve immediately, garnished with watercress.

SERVES 4
as part of a tapas meal

3 garlic cloves
4 tbsp Spanish olive oil
1 Spanish onion, halved and finely chopped
14 oz/400 g canned cannellini beans, drained and rinsed
4 tomatoes, diced
4 thick slices country bread
10 oz/280 g cooked shelled shrimp
salt and pepper
watercress, to garnish

cheese & sun-dried tomato toasts

SERVES 4
as part of a tapas meal

2 small French loaves
¾ cup sun-dried tomato paste
1 small ball fresh buffalo
   mozzarella
1½ tsp dried oregano
2–3 tbsp olive oil
pepper

Preheat the broiler on a medium–high setting and preheat the oven to 425°F/220°C. Slice the loaves diagonally and discard the end pieces. Toast the slices on both sides under the broiler until golden.

Spread one side of each toast with the sun-dried tomato paste and top with mozzarella. Sprinkle with oregano and season with pepper to taste.

Put the toasts on a large baking sheet and drizzle with oil. Bake in the preheated oven for 5 minutes, or until the cheese is melted and bubbling. Remove the toasts from the oven and let stand for 5 minutes before serving.

avocado shrimp toasts

SERVES 4
as part of a tapas meal

2 cups peeled cooked shrimp,
   thawed if frozen
2 tbsp cornstarch
1 egg white
grated zest of 1 lemon
1 celery stalk, finely chopped
2 tbsp chopped fresh parsley
4 tbsp snipped fresh chives
4 medium-thick slices good
   white bread
1/4 cup butter, melted
2 avocados
1 tbsp lemon juice
1/2 tsp Dijon mustard (or other
   type, to taste)
1 tbsp tarragon
3 tbsp olive oil
salt and pepper
fresh tarragon sprigs,
   to garnish

Finely chop the shrimp in a food processor. Add the cornstarch, egg white, and seasoning, and pulse once or twice to mix to a coarse paste. Do not over-process the mixture or it will become too thin. Transfer to a bowl and mix in the lemon zest, celery, parsley, and chives.

Preheat the broiler to medium–high. Brush the bread lightly with butter on both sides and toast on the rack in the broiler pan for 2 minutes on each side. The pan must not be too near the heat.

Reduce the heat to medium–low. Trim the very edges of the crusts off the toasts and divide the shrimp mixture among the toasts, spreading it out evenly to cover the bread completely. Broil for 1 minute, until the mixture is lightly set, then brush with the remaining butter. Cook for 3–4 minutes, until set and golden.

Halve, pit, peel, and dice the avocados. Whisk the lemon juice with the mustard, tarragon, and seasoning. Gradually whisk in the oil.

Cut the cooked toasts into quarters and place on warmed plates. Top with the avocado and the lemon dressing, garnish with the tarragon sprigs, and serve.

roman dip with anchovy circles

Put the egg in a saucepan, then cover with cold water and slowly bring to a boil. Reduce the heat and simmer gently for 10 minutes. Immediately drain the egg and rinse under cold running water to cool. Gently tap the egg to crack the shell and leave until cold.

When the egg is cold, crack the shell all over and remove it. Put the egg in a food processor and add the olives, 2 of the anchovy fillets, the crushed garlic, capers, paprika, and brandy and process to a coarse paste. With the motor running, very slowly add 1 tablespoon of the reserved oil from the anchovies and the extra virgin olive oil in a thin, steady stream. Season the dip with pepper to taste.

Transfer the dip to a small serving bowl, then cover and chill in the refrigerator until ready to serve. To make the anchovy circles, put the remaining anchovy fillets, remaining reserved oil from the anchovies, and garlic clove in a mortar and, using a pestle, pound together to a paste. Turn the paste into a bowl, then cover and chill in the refrigerator until ready to serve.

When ready to serve, preheat the broiler to high. Cut the bread into 1-inch/2.5-cm slices and toast under the broiler until golden brown on both sides. Spread the anchovy paste very thinly on the toasted bread circles and serve with the dip.

SERVES 12
as part of a tapas meal

1 egg
scant 1 cup pitted black Spanish olives
1³/₄ oz/50 g canned anchovy fillets in olive oil, drained and oil reserved
2 garlic cloves, 1 crushed and 1 peeled but kept whole
1 tbsp capers
¹/₂ tsp hot or sweet smoked Spanish paprika
1 tbsp Spanish brandy or sherry
4 tbsp Spanish extra virgin olive oil
1 small French loaf
pepper

onion & olive circles

SERVES 4–8
as part of a tapas meal

2 tbsp Spanish olive oil
1 onion, thinly sliced
1 garlic clove, finely chopped
2 tsp chopped fresh thyme
1 small French loaf
1 tbsp tapenade or butter
8 canned anchovy fillets in oil,
   drained
12 green Spanish olives stuffed
   with almonds or onion, halved
salt and pepper

Heat the olive oil in a heavy-bottom skillet. Add the onion and garlic and cook over low heat, stirring occasionally, for 15 minutes, or until golden brown and very soft. Stir in the thyme and season with salt and pepper to taste.

Meanwhile, cut off and discard the crusty ends of the bread, then cut the loaf into 8 slices. Toast on both sides, then spread one side with the tapenade.

Pile the onion mixture onto the slices of toast and top each slice with an anchovy fillet and some olive halves. Serve hot.

anchovy rolls

SERVES 4
as part of a tapas meal

butter, for greasing and
  spreading
8 salted anchovies
¼ cup milk
4 slices white bread, crusts
  removed
1 tbsp Dijon mustard
2 tbsp grated Manchego or
  cheddar cheese

Preheat the oven to 425°F/220°C. Lightly grease a baking sheet. Place the anchovies in a small, shallow dish and pour over the milk. Let soak for 10–15 minutes. Drain, discarding the milk, and pat dry with paper towels.

Spread each bread slice with butter and then with mustard. Sprinkle with the grated cheese. Divide the anchovies among the bread slices and roll up.

Place on the baking sheet, seam-side down, and bake in the preheated oven for 6–7 minutes. Let cool slightly, then serve.

salads on bread

To make the potato salad, peel the potatoes as soon as they are cool enough to handle, then cut into 1/4-inch/5-mm dice. Toss with the vinegar and season with salt and pepper to taste. Let cool completely. Stir in the mayonnaise, then fold in the eggs and scallions. Taste and adjust the seasoning. Cut the bread on a slight diagonal into 12 slices, 1/4 inch/5 mm thick. Mound the salad onto the bread.

To make the tuna salad, flake the tuna into a bowl. Stir in the mayonnaise, then fold in the eggs, tomato, lemon rind, and cayenne pepper. Taste and adjust the seasoning. Cut the bread on a slight diagonal into 12 slices, 1/4 inch/5 mm thick. Mound the salad on the bread, then top with anchovy fillets.

**each salad SERVES 6
as part of a tapas meal**

potato salad
7 oz/200 g new potatoes, scrubbed and boiled
1/2 tbsp white wine vinegar
3–4 tbsp mayonnaise
2 hard-cooked eggs, shelled and finely chopped
2 scallions, white and green parts finely chopped
1 large French loaf
salt and pepper

tuna salad
7 oz/200 g canned tuna in olive oil, drained
4 tbsp mayonnaise
2 hard-cooked eggs, shelled and finely chopped
1 tomato, roasted and peeled, seeded, and very finely chopped
2 tsp grated lemon rind, or to taste
cayenne pepper, to taste
1 large French loaf
12 anchovy fillets in oil, drained, to garnish
salt and pepper

flatbread with vegetables & clams

SERVES 4–6
as part of a tapas meal

2 tbsp Spanish extra virgin
   olive oil
4 large garlic cloves, crushed
2 large onions, thinly sliced
10 pimientos del piquillo,
   drained, patted dry, and
   thinly sliced
9 oz/250 g shelled baby clams
   in brine (weight in jar),
   drained and rinsed
salt and pepper

bread dough
$2^{2}/_{3}$ cups white bread flour,
   plus extra for dusting
1 envelope active dry yeast
1 tsp salt
$^{1}/_{2}$ tsp sugar
1 tbsp Spanish olive oil, plus
   extra for oiling
1 tbsp dry white wine
1 cup warm water

To make the bread dough, stir the flour, yeast, salt, and sugar together in a bowl, making a well in the center. Add the olive oil and wine to the water, then pour $^{1}/_{4}$ cup of the liquid into the well. Gradually mix in the flour from the sides, adding the remaining liquid if necessary, until a soft dough forms.

Turn out the dough onto a lightly floured counter and knead until smooth. Shape the dough into a ball. Wash the bowl and rub the inside with olive oil. Return the dough to the bowl and roll it around until lightly coated in oil. Cover the bowl tightly with plastic wrap and let stand in a warm place until the dough doubles in size.

Heat the olive oil in a large, heavy-bottom skillet over medium heat. Reduce the heat and add the garlic and onions and cook slowly, stirring frequently, for 25 minutes, or until the onions are golden brown but not burned.

Preheat the oven to 450°F/230°C. Transfer the onions to a bowl and let cool. Add the pimiento del piquillo strips and the clams to the bowl and stir together. Reserve.

Punch down the dough and knead quickly on a lightly floured counter. Cover it with the upturned bowl and let stand for 10 minutes, which will make it easier to roll out.

Heavily flour a $12^{3}/_{4} \times 12^{3}/_{4}$-inch/$32 \times 32$-cm shallow baking sheet. Roll out the dough to make a $13^{1}/_{2}$-inch/34-cm square and transfer it to the baking sheet, rolling the edges to form a thin rim. Prick the base all over with a fork.

Spread the topping evenly over the dough and season with salt and pepper to taste. Bake in the preheated oven for 25 minutes, or until the rim is golden brown and the onion tips are slightly tinged. Transfer to a wire rack to cool completely. Cut into 12–16 slices.

artichoke & pimiento flatbread

SERVES 4–6
as part of a tapas meal

4 tbsp Spanish olive oil, plus
    extra for oiling
2 large onions, thinly sliced
2 garlic cloves, finely chopped
14 oz/400 g canned artichoke
    hearts, drained and quartered
11¼ oz/320 g bottled or canned
    pimientos del piquillo,
    drained and thinly sliced
scant ¼ cup pitted black
    Spanish olives (optional)
salt and pepper

bread dough
heaping 2¾ cups white bread
    flour, plus extra for dusting
1½ tsp active dry yeast
1 tsp salt
½ tsp superfine sugar
¾ cup warm water
3 tbsp Spanish olive oil

To make the bread dough, put the flour, yeast, salt, and sugar in a large bowl and make a well in the center. Mix the water and oil together in a pitcher and pour into the well, then gradually mix in the flour from the side. Using your hands, mix together to form a soft dough that leaves the side of the bowl clean.

Turn out the dough onto a lightly floured counter and knead for 10 minutes, or until smooth and elastic and no longer sticky. Shape the dough into a ball and put in a clean bowl. Cover with a clean, damp dish towel and leave in a warm place for 1 hour, or until the dough has risen and doubled in size.

Meanwhile, heat 3 tablespoons of the oil in a large skillet, then add the onions and cook over medium heat, stirring occasionally, for 10 minutes, or until golden brown. Add the garlic and cook, stirring, for 30 seconds, or until softened. Let cool. When cool, stir in the artichoke hearts and pimientos del piquillo, then season with salt and pepper to taste.

Preheat the oven to 400°F/200°C. Oil a large cookie sheet. Turn out the risen dough onto a lightly floured counter and knead lightly for 2–3 minutes to knock out the air. Roll out the dough to a 12-inch/30-cm square and transfer to the prepared cookie sheet.

Brush the remaining oil over the dough and spread the artichoke and pimiento mixture on top. Sprinkle over the olives, if using. Bake in the preheated oven for 20–25 minutes, or until golden brown and crisp. Cut into 12 slices and serve hot or warm.

sun-dried tomato toasts
with goat cheese

Preheat the oven to 400°F/200°C. Generously oil a cookie sheet. To make the toasts, very finely chop the tomatoes and put in a bowl. Add the reserved oil from the tomatoes and the garlic and mix together well.

Slice the bread into 1/2-inch/1-cm thick slices and spread with the tomato mixture. Put on the prepared cookie sheet and bake in the preheated oven for 10 minutes, or until golden brown and crisp. Let cool on a wire rack.

To make the dip, put the goat cheese in a food processor. With the motor running, add 1 tablespoon of the oil, drop by drop. Using a spatula, scrape down the side of the bowl. With the motor running again, very slowly add the remaining oil and the lemon juice in a thin, steady stream. Add the garlic and paprika and process until well mixed.

Stir the olives and parsley into the dip. Turn the dip into a small serving bowl, then cover and chill in the refrigerator for at least 1 hour before serving.

Serve the dip accompanied by the toasts.

SERVES 6
as part of a tapas meal

2 tbsp Spanish extra virgin olive oil, plus extra for oiling
8 oz/225 g soft goat cheese
2 tsp freshly squeezed lemon juice
2 garlic cloves, crushed
1 tsp hot or sweet smoked Spanish paprika
heaping 1/8 cup pitted green Spanish olives, finely chopped
1 tbsp chopped fresh flat-leaf parsley

sun-dried tomato toasts
1 3/4 oz/50 g sun-dried tomatoes in oil, drained and 3 tbsp oil reserved
1 garlic clove, crushed
1 long French bread

fresh mint & bean pâté

SERVES 12
as part of a tapas meal

1 lb 12 oz/800 g fresh fava
    beans in their pods, shelled
    to give about 12 oz/350 g
8 oz/225 g soft goat cheese
1 garlic clove, crushed
2 scallions, finely chopped
1 tbsp Spanish extra virgin olive
    oil, plus extra to serve
grated lemon rind
2 tbsp lemon juice
about 60 large fresh mint
    leaves, 1/2 oz/15 g
    in total
12 slices French bread
salt and pepper

Bring a saucepan of lightly salted water to a boil, add the beans and cook for 8–10 minutes, or until tender. Drain well and let cool. When the beans are cool enough to handle, slip off their skins and put the beans in a food processor. This is a laborious task, but worth doing if you have the time. This quantity will take about 15 minutes to skin.

Add the goat cheese, garlic, scallions, oil, lemon rind and juice, and mint leaves to the fava beans and process until well mixed. Season the pâté with salt and pepper to taste. Turn into a bowl, cover, then chill in the refrigerator for at least 1 hour before serving.

To serve, preheat the broiler to high. Toast the bread slices under the broiler until golden brown on both sides. Drizzle a little oil over the toasted bread slices, then spread the pâté on top and serve immediately.

eggplant & bell pepper dip

SERVES 6–8
as part of a tapas meal

2 large eggplants
2 red bell peppers
4 tbsp Spanish olive oil
2 garlic cloves, coarsely
   chopped
grated rind and juice of
   $1/2$ lemon
1 tbsp chopped cilantro, plus
   extra sprigs to garnish
$1/2$–1 tsp paprika
salt and pepper
bread or toast, to serve

Preheat the oven to 375°F/190°C. Prick the skins of the eggplants and bell peppers all over with a fork and brush with 1 tablespoon of the olive oil. Place on a baking sheet and bake in the preheated oven for 45 minutes, or until the skins are beginning to turn black, the flesh of the eggplant is very soft, and the bell peppers are deflated.

Place the cooked vegetables in a bowl and cover tightly with a clean, damp dish towel. Alternatively, place the vegetables in a plastic bag and let stand for about 15 minutes, or until cool enough to handle.

When the vegetables have cooled, cut the eggplants in half lengthwise, carefully scoop out the flesh, and discard the skin. Cut the eggplant flesh into large chunks. Remove and discard the stem, core, and seeds from the bell peppers and cut the flesh into large pieces.

Heat the remaining olive oil in a skillet. Add the eggplant and bell pepper and cook for 5 minutes. Add the garlic and cook for 30 seconds.

Turn the contents of the skillet onto paper towels to drain, then transfer to a food processor. Add the lemon rind and juice, the chopped cilantro, the paprika, and salt and pepper to taste, then process until a speckled puree is formed.

Transfer the eggplant and bell pepper dip to a serving bowl. Serve warm, at room temperature, or let cool for 30 minutes, then let chill in the refrigerator for at least 1 hour and serve cold. Garnish with cilantro sprigs and accompany with thick slices of bread or toast for dipping.

wild mushroom & aïoli toasts

Heat the oil in a large skillet, then add the garlic and cook over medium heat, stirring, for 30 seconds, or until softened. Increase the heat to high, then add the mushrooms and cook, stirring continuously, until the mushrooms are coated in the oil and all the oil has been absorbed.

Reduce the heat to low and cook for 2–3 minutes, or until all the juices have been released from the mushrooms. Add the sherry, increase the heat to high again and cook, stirring frequently, for 3–4 minutes until the liquid has evaporated. Stir in the parsley and season with salt and pepper to taste.

Meanwhile, preheat the broiler to high. Toast the bread slices under the broiler until lightly golden brown on both sides.

Spread the aïoli on top of each toast and top with the cooked mushrooms. Carefully transfer the toasts to a broiler rack and cook under the broiler until the aïoli starts to bubble. Serve hot.

SERVES 6
as part of a tapas meal

5 tbsp Spanish olive oil
2 large garlic cloves, finely
 chopped
1 lb/450 g wild or cultivated
 mushrooms, sliced
2 tbsp dry Spanish sherry
4 tbsp chopped fresh
 flat-leaf parsley
12 slices long, thick crusty
 bread
8 tbsp Aïoli (see page 58)
salt and pepper

roasted red bell peppers on garlic toasts

SERVES 4
as part of a tapas meal

4 thin slices white country
   bread
5 tbsp Spanish olive oil
2 large garlic cloves, crushed
3 large red bell peppers
pepper
chopped fresh flat-leaf parsley,
   to garnish

Preheat the oven to 450°F/230°C. To make the garlic toasts, halve each bread slice. Put 3 tablespoons of the oil in a bowl and stir in the garlic. Brush each side of the bread slice halves with the oil mixture and transfer to a cookie sheet. Bake in the preheated oven for 10–15 minutes, or until crisp and golden brown. Let cool on paper towels.

Reduce the oven temperature to 400°F/200°C. Brush the red bell peppers with the remaining oil and put in a roasting pan. Roast in the oven for 30 minutes, then turn over and roast for an additional 10 minutes, or until the skins have blistered and blackened.

Using a slotted spoon, transfer the roasted peppers to a plastic bag for 15 minutes, or until cool enough to handle.

Carefully peel away the skin from the bell peppers. Halve them and remove the stems, cores, and seeds, then cut each one into neat, thin strips.

To serve, arrange the bell pepper strips on top of the garlic toasts. Season with pepper to taste and sprinkle with chopped parsley to garnish.

tomato bread

SERVES 4
as part of a tapas meal

4 slices French bread
2 ripe tomatoes, halved
1 garlic clove, finely chopped
   (optional)
2 tbsp Spanish olive oil
   (optional)

If the bread is soft, toast it under a preheated broiler until lightly golden on both sides. Rub each slice of bread with half a fresh juicy tomato. If using, sprinkle over the chopped garlic and drizzle the oil over the top.

asparagus rolls

Preheat the oven to 375°F/190°C and lightly grease a baking sheet. If woody, peel the asparagus stems, then tie the spears loosely together with clean kitchen string. Blanch in a tall saucepan of boiling water for 3–5 minutes. Drain and refresh under cold running water. Drain again and pat dry with paper towels.

Lightly flatten the slices of bread with a rolling pin. Mix half of the butter, and all of the parsley, and orange rind together in a bowl and season with salt and pepper to taste. Spread the flavored butter over the bread slices.

Place an asparagus spear near one side of a bread slice and roll up. Repeat with the remaining asparagus spears and bread. Place the asparagus rolls, seam-side down, on the baking sheet.

Melt the remaining butter in a small saucepan, then brush it over the asparagus rolls. Bake in the preheated oven for 15 minutes, or until crisp and golden brown. Let cool slightly, then serve warm.

SERVES 8
as part of a tapas meal

1/2 cup butter, softened, plus
    extra for greasing
8 asparagus spears, trimmed
8 slices white bread, crusts
    removed
1 tbsp chopped fresh parsley
finely grated rind of 1 orange
salt and pepper

spinach & tomato pizzas

SERVES 16
as part of a tapas meal

2 tbsp Spanish olive oil, plus
    extra for brushing and
    drizzling
1 onion, finely chopped
1 garlic clove, finely chopped
14 oz/400 g canned chopped
    tomatoes
4$^{1}/_{2}$ oz/125 g fresh baby spinach
2 tbsp pine nuts
salt and pepper

pizza dough
scant $^{1}/_{2}$ cup warm water
$^{1}/_{2}$ tsp active dry yeast
pinch of sugar
1$^{1}/_{3}$ cups white bread flour,
    plus extra for dusting
$^{1}/_{2}$ tsp salt

To make the pizza dough, measure the water into a small bowl. Sprinkle in the dried yeast and sugar and let stand in a warm place for 10–15 minutes, or until frothy.

Meanwhile, sift the flour and salt into a large bowl. Make a well in the center and pour in the yeast liquid, then mix together with a spoon. Using your hands, work the mixture until it leaves the sides of the bowl clean.

Turn out the dough onto a lightly floured counter and knead for 10 minutes, or until smooth and elastic and no longer sticky. Shape into a ball and put in a clean bowl. Cover with a clean, damp dish towel and let stand in a warm place for 1 hour, or until it has risen and doubled in size.

To make the topping, heat the oil in a large, heavy-bottom skillet. Add the onion and cook for 5 minutes, or until softened but not browned. Add the garlic and cook for an additional 30 seconds. Stir in the tomatoes and cook for 5 minutes, letting it bubble and stirring occasionally, until reduced to a thick mixture. Add the spinach leaves and cook, stirring, until they have wilted slightly. Season with salt and pepper to taste.

While the dough is rising, preheat the oven to 400°F/200°C. Brush several baking sheets with oil. Turn out the dough onto a lightly floured counter and knead well for 2–3 minutes to knock out the air bubbles.

Roll out the dough very, very thinly and, using a 2$^{1}/_{2}$-inch/6-cm plain, round cutter, cut out 32 circles. Place on the prepared baking sheets.

Spread each base with the spinach mixture to cover, then sprinkle the pine nuts over the top. Drizzle a little oil over each pizza. Bake in the preheated oven for 10–15 minutes, or until the edges of the dough are golden brown. Serve the spinach and tomato pizzas hot.

chorizo pizza

**SERVES 4–6
as part of a tapas meal**

6 tomatoes, sliced
2 onions, finely chopped
12 black olives
4 serrano ham slices
10 ready-to-eat chorizo
 sausage slices
2 tbsp chopped mixed fresh
 herbs
2 oz/55 g Tronchon or
 mozzarella cheese, thinly
 sliced
$1/4$ cup olive oil
salt and pepper

pizza dough
1 package fresh yeast
$1^2/3$ cups all-purpose flour, plus
 extra for dusting
1 cup lukewarm water
pinch of salt
$1/4$ cup olive oil

First make the pizza dough. Mix the yeast with $1/3$ cup of the flour and the water in a bowl. Let stand for 10 minutes.

Meanwhile, sift the remaining flour with the salt into a large bowl and make a well in the center. Add the yeast mixture and the oil. Using an electric mixer, mix well for 5–10 minutes. Cover with a clean dish towel and let stand in a warm place until the dough has doubled in size.

Preheat the oven to 425°F/220°C and place a baking sheet in the oven to warm. Pat out the pizza dough into an 11–12-inch/28–30-cm circle on a lightly floured counter and make a slightly raised rim around the edge.

Arrange the tomato slices on top of the pizza dough and season with salt to taste, then cover with the onion. Add the olives, ham, and chorizo, then season with pepper to taste and sprinkle over the herbs. Top with the cheese slices and drizzle with the olive oil.

Carefully transfer the pizza to the preheated baking sheet and bake in the preheated oven for 30 minutes, or until the cheese has melted and is bubbling and the rim has lightly browned. Cut into wedges and serve.